FOOTBALL
QUIZ
BOOK

HarperCollins Publishers
Westerhill Road
Bishopbriggs
Glasgow
G64 2QT

First Edition 2012

Reprint 10 9 8 7 6 5 4 3 2 1 0

© HarperCollins Publishers 2012

ISBN 978-0-00-747996-2

Collins® is a registered trademark of
HarperCollins Publishers Limited

www.collinslanguage.com

A catalogue record for this book is
available from the British Library

Typeset by Davidson Publishing
Solutions, Glasgow

Printed in Great Britain by Clays Ltd,
St Ives plc

Acknowledgements
We would like to thank those authors
and publishers who kindly gave
permission for copyright material
to be used in the Collins Corpus.
We would also like to thank Times
Newspapers Ltd for providing
valuable data.

AUTHOR
Chris Bradshaw

EDITOR
Gerry Breslin
Freddy Chick

FOR THE PUBLISHER
Lucy Cooper
Julianna Dunn
Kerry Ferguson
Elaine Higgleton

Introduction

It's a sad thing to think that football was only formalised in terms of rules in the nineteenth century. It makes all the periods of history that went before look deprived and largely irrelevant. Since its arrival on earth though, the beautiful game has been making up for lost time, quickly establishing itself as the best and most important thing ever to happen to mankind. You can keep your Romans, Vikings, legends or what have you: Football is the greatest saga the world has ever seen. As Bill Shankly put it:

> 'Some people think football is a matter of life and death. I don't like that attitude. I can assure them it is much more serious than that.'

From Reykjavik to Rio, hundreds of millions of fans head to the stadium, the pub, or turn on the TV or radio each weekend and lose themselves in the epic drama of the football season. When not actually watching football, they listen to the media storm that is always raging about the game. Week in, week out, those brave chroniclers add new chapters to the story of football: championship run-ins, rising young stars, incompetent managers, biased referees, incredible performances, woeful displays, sackings and transfers, red cards and wonder goals.

Collins Football Quiz Book tests your knowledge of the story of football and how well you really know the game. There are quizzes on every major European and South American league, on all the domestic cups, on the Champions League and UEFA, international competitions, managers and players. It's the perfect way of whiling away the hours while football isn't being played.

The quizzes

The quizzes are grouped according to how tricky they are.
There's easy, then medium and then difficult quizzes.

Easy

If you're footie mad, then these quizzes are going to be a walk in
the park. You should be finishing them off every day of the week.
There are a couple of tougher questions in the mix that might
even be labelled as 'challenging' by some judges. These have been
included to add the frisson of mental sweat to an easy round.

Medium

These are the ones that will have you battling for the point.
Lesser football quizzers might find themselves getting skinned
by a couple and looking a right fool. Remember the basics and
you'll be fine though: keep your eye on the ball, keep a nice tight
line, and 'if in doubt, put it out'.

Difficult

These are the rounds that make legends. Anyone who can
answer these must know almost as much as John Motson. You'll
need to show endurance, guts and a footballing brain like Brian
Clough's to come out on top of these.

The answers

The answers to each quiz are printed at the end of the following
quiz. For example, the answers to Quiz 1-Pot Luck appear at the
bottom of Quiz 2-Premier League. The exception to this rule is
the last quiz in every level. The answers to these quizzes appear
at the end of the very first quiz in the level.

Running a quiz

Collins Football Quiz Book is only half-finished. (Wait! Don't
demand a refund yet, read on!) People don't go to the theatre
to sit and read a script. Likewise, the quizzes in this book need
someone to read them out. That's you.

If you're just quizzing your family during a car journey, or your mates during half-time, then there's probably no need to put in lots of preparation. If you're planning on using this book to run a more organized and formal quiz however, there are a few things you need to get right before you start.

❖ Rehearse: don't just pick this book up and read out the questions cold. Go through all the quizzes you're going to use by yourself beforehand. Note down all the questions (notes look better in a quiz environment than reading from a book) and answers. Although every effort has been made to ensure that all the answers in *Collins Football Quiz Book* are correct, despite our best endeavours, mistakes may still appear. If you see an answer you are not sure is right, or if you think there is more than one possible answer, then check.

❖ Paper and writing implements: do yourself a favour and prepare enough sheets of paper for everyone to write on. The aim of the game here is to stop the mad impulse certain people feel to 'help'. They will spend ten minutes running around looking for 'scrap' paper, probably ripping up your latest novel in the process. The same problem applies to pens. Ideally, have enough for everyone. Remember, though, that over half of them will be lost forever once you've given them out. You can use the 'Keeping Score' pages at the back of the book to record the quiz scores for each team or person.

❖ Prizes: everyone likes a prize. Since this is a football quiz book, your audience will probably not understand the concept of a competition without one. No matter how small, it's best to have one on offer.

Good luck! We hope you enjoy *Collins Football Quiz Book*.

Contents

Easy Quizzes

Medium Quizzes

Difficult Quizzes

EASY QUIZZES

Quiz 1: Pot Luck

1. Prenton Park is the home ground of which Football League club?

2. Gareth Bale started his professional career at which club?

3. Which former Germany and Liverpool midfielder's autobiography is called The Didi Man?

4. Who were the last winners of the old First Division before it became the Premier League?

5. Who was appointed manager of the 2012 Great Britain Olympic team?

6. Which team scored three own goals in a 6-1 FA Cup thrashing at Liverpool in 2012?

7. Maine Road was the former ground of which club?

8. Who was the first player to be knighted for his services to the game?

9. What is the largest club ground in England?

10. Harry Redknapp has managed which five English League clubs?

11. Who were the two Chelsea goalscorers in the 2012 FA Cup final?

12. Which football-inspired game takes its name from the Latin name of a bird of prey?

13. What is the name of the park that divides Anfield from Goodison Park?

14. What is the oldest professional football club in the world?

15. How many words of English did Fabio Capello say he needed to communicate with his players?

EASY

16. Who did Alex Ferguson succeed as manager of Manchester United?

17. Oscar winner Richard Attenborough is a life-president at which club?

18. Who is the only player to play a full international for England whose surname begins with Z?

19. Which team has won the most Italian Serie A titles?
    a) AC Milan
    b) Inter Milan
    c) Juventus

20. The 2010 World Cup final was held in which city?
    a) Cape Town
    b) Johannesburg
    c) Pretoria

Answers to Quiz 33: Pot Luck

1. Mario Balotelli
2. Newcastle United
3. Wayne Rooney
4. A virgin
5. Yeovil Town
6. Swansea City
7. Fraizer Campbell
8. Birmingham City
9. Highbury
10. St Johnstone
11. Inter Milan
12. Liverpool, Leeds, Manchester City, Blackburn Rovers and Cardiff City
13. Noel Gallagher
14. Dave Beasant
15. Dave Mackay, Brian Clough and Billy Davies
16. Chris Baird
17. Jermaine Pennant
18. Paul Cooper
19. 6 seconds
20. Ukraine

Quiz 2: Premier League

1. In what year was the Premier League formed?

2. Which seven clubs have been ever-presents in the Premier League?

3. In what season did Blackburn win the Premier League title?

4. Which team, in 2009/10, became the first to score over 100 Premier League goals in a season?

5. Who was the only player to play in all of the first 20 Premier League seasons?

6. Which team attracted the lowest crowd in the history of the Premier League?

7. Who was the first African player to notch up 100 Premier League goals?

8. Who scored the Premier League's first goal?

9. Who did Roberto Martinez succeed as manager of Wigan Athletic?

10. What animal appears on the logo of the Premier League?

11. Who scored more Premier League goals – Dennis Bergkamp or Jimmy Floyd Hasselbaink?

12. Which Irish international has provided plenty of assists for Stoke with his huge throw-ins?

13. What flower features on the badge of Blackburn Rovers?

14. Who was the only goalkeeper to make the 2011/12 PFA Player of the Year shortlist?

15. Which brothers played for Newcastle against Chelsea in May 2011?

16. Which goalkeeper has made the most Premier League appearances?

17. How many English managers have won the Premier League since its inception?

18. In what season did Arsenal last win the Premier League?

19. Excluding the UK and Ireland, which country has provided the most Premier League players?
    a) France
    b) Holland
    c) Sweden

20. Who is the Premier League's all-time leading scorer?
    a) Andy Cole
    b) Thierry Henry
    c) Alan Shearer

Answers to Quiz 1: Pot Luck

1. Tranmere
2. Southampton
3. Dietmar Hamman
4. Leeds United
5. Stuart Pearce
6. Brighton and Hove Albion
7. Manchester City
8. Sir Stanley Matthews
9. Old Trafford
10. Bournemouth, West Ham, Portsmouth (twice), Southampton and Tottenham
11. Ramires and Drogba
12. Subbuteo
13. Stanley Park
14. Notts County
15. 100
16. Ron Atkinson
17. Chelsea
18. Bobby Zamora
19. Juventus
20. Johannesburg

Quiz 3: Pot Luck

1. Which two clubs gained automatic promotion from the Championship in 2011/12?

2. Which England player had a goal disallowed in the 2010 World Cup against Germany despite the ball clearly crossing the line?

3. True or false – a player can be offside if he receives the ball direct from a throw-in?

4. Only one league team in England or Scotland has the letter J in its name. Which one?

5. Which team has spent the most consecutive seasons in England's top flight?

6. Who holds the record for the most goals in a single top flight season?

7. Which club won the French league seven years in a row in the 2000s?

8. What is the South American equivalent of the Champions League?

9. Which on-loan goalkeeper scored an injury-time winner to preserve Carlisle's Football League status in the last game of the 1999 season?

10. The song I'm Forever Blowing Bubbles is associated with which club?

11. Prime Minister David Cameron and Prince William are both fans of which club?

12. Which Italian legend was nicknamed The Divine Ponytail?

13. Who was Chelsea's last English manager?

14. Which English team are nicknamed The Rams?

15. What was broadcast for the first time on 22 August 1964?

16. Boleslaw is the middle name of which legendary goalkeeper?

17. Who was named England caretaker manager after Fabio Capello's departure?

18. Which England striker's middle name is Ivanhoe?

19. The beautifully coiffeured Marouanne Fallaini plays international football for which country?
    a) Belgium
    b) Denmark
    c) Sweden

20. What is the nickname of the Real Madrid versus Barcelona derby?
    a) El Clasico
    b) El Superbo
    c) El Ultimo

Answers to Quiz 2: Premier League

1. 1992
2. Manchester United, Arsenal, Liverpool, Chelsea, Aston Villa, Tottenham and Everton
3. 1994/95
4. Chelsea
5. Ryan Giggs
6. Wimbledon
7. Didier Drogba
8. Brian Deane
9. Steve Bruce
10. Lion
11. Jimmy Floyd Hasselbaink
12. Rory Delap
13. Red rose
14. Joe Hart
15. Shola and Sammy Ameobi
16. David James
17. None
18. 2003/04
19. France
20. Alan Shearer

Quiz 4: The FA Cup

EASY

1. Who won FA Cup-winner's medals in 2002, 2003, 2005, 2007, 2009, 2010 and 2012?

2. David James has appeared in FA Cup finals for which three clubs?

3. Alex Ferguson won his first trophy in England when Manchester United beat which club in the 1990 FA Cup final?

4. What is taken to every FA Cup final but isn't used?

5. Which team won the last FA Cup final at the old Wembley and the first at the new?

6. Who did Manchester City beat in the 2011 FA Cup final?

7. In what round do Premier League teams enter the FA Cup?

8. Which team reached the final in 1978, 1979 and 1980?

9. Who was the first foreign manager to win the FA Cup?

10. Which two teams were involved in the first FA Cup final penalty shoot-out?

11. Which team won the Cup in 1988, only 11 years after they joined the Football League?

12. Who are the only team from outside England to win the FA Cup?

13. Six FA Cup finals were held at Cardiff's Millennium Stadium, which three clubs won all six finals?

14. Which team won their only FA Cup in 1987?

15. Why did Manchester United not take part in the 2000 FA Cup?

EASY

16. Who scored after just 43 seconds in Chelsea's 1997 win over Middlesbrough?

17. Which Nigerian international scored the winner in Portsmouth's 2008 victory over Cardiff?

18. Which brewery took up the sponsorship of the FA Cup in 2011?

19. In what year did Ipswich Town win their only FA Cup?
    a) 1977
    b) 1978
    c) 1979

20. Which manager has won the most FA Cups?
    a) Alex Ferguson
    b) Bob Paisley
    c) Arsene Wenger

Answers to Quiz 3: Pot Luck

1. Reading and Southampton	11. Aston Villa
2. Frank Lampard	12. Roberto Baggio
3. False	13. Glenn Hoddle
4. St Johnstone	14. Derby County
5. Arsenal	15. Match of the Day
6. Dixie Dean with 60	16. Peter Schmeichel
7. Lyon	17. Stuart Pearce
8. Copa Libertadores	18. Emile Heskey
9. Jimmy Glass	19. Belgium
10. West Ham United	20. El Clasico

Quiz 5: Pot Luck

1. Who beat Bolton 5-0 to reach the 2011 FA Cup final?

2. Actor Sean Bean is a fan of which Yorkshire club?

3. Which manager is nicknamed The Special One?

4. Paul Gascoigne played for which Italian club?

5. Alan 'The Apprentice' Sugar was the chairman of which club?

6. Which Premier League manager is nicknamed 'The Professor'?

7. True or false – Newcastle United's home shirts were once red and white stripes?

8. Who helped his country qualify for the 2010 World Cup by using the so-called 'la Main de dieu'?

9. Who did Chelsea beat 5-1 in the 2012 FA Cup semifinal?

10. Sampdoria are based in which Italian city?

11. The name of which English club starts with five successive consonants?

12. The number 25 shirt at Chelsea was retired in honour of which player?

13. Chris Hughton was the manager of which club before taking the reins at Birmingham City?

14. Which manager steered Charlton to promotion from League One in 2012?

15. Which team has won the most German Bundesliga titles?

16. Who famously said of Manchester United, 'I would love it if we beat them, love it!'?

EASY

17. West Ham retired the number 6 shirt in honour of which player?

18. The names of which six teams in the top four divisions of English football end in the letter E?

19. Which country lost the 2010 World Cup final?
    a) Germany
    b) Holland
    c) Italy

20. What is the name of Hibernian's home ground?
    a) Christmas Road
    b) Easter Road
    c) Advent Road

Answers to Quiz 4: The FA Cup

1. Ashley Cole
2. Liverpool, Aston Villa and Portsmouth
3. Crystal Palace
4. The ribbons for the losing team
5. Chelsea
6. Stoke City
7. 3rd
8. Arsenal
9. Ruud Gullit
10. Arsenal and Manchester United
11. Wimbledon
12. Cardiff City
13. Arsenal, Liverpool and Manchester United
14. Coventry City
15. They were participating in the World Club Championship
16. Roberto di Matteo
17. Nwankwo Kanu
18. Budweiser
19. 1978
20. Alex Ferguson

Quiz 6: England

1. Who scored England's goals in their 1966 World Cup final win?

2. Who is the youngest player to play for England?

3. Which African country did England beat in the 1990 World Cup quarterfinal?

4. Who scored England's goals in their famous 4-1 demolition of Holland in Euro 96?

5. Which manager led England to the semifinals of the 1990 World Cup?

6. Who scored the goals in England's 5-1 win over Germany in Munich in 2001?

7. At 42 years, 103 days, who is the oldest player to represent England?

8. Which Nottingham Forest defender was the first black player to play for England?

9. Who missed the penalty in England's shoot-out loss to Germany in Euro 1996?

10. England suffered their biggest ever World Cup defeat in 2010. Who were their opponents and what was the score?

11. How many games did England lose in the qualification group for Euro 2012?

12. Who is the tallest player ever to play for England?

13. Which team knocked England out of the World Cup in 2002?

14. Who were England's opponents in their first international match?

15. Who did Fabio Capello succeed as England manager?

16. Who, in a game against China in 1996, became the first brothers to represent England since Jack and Bobby Charlton?

17. Who was the England manager at the 1966 World Cup?

18. Who is England's most capped player?

19. How many goals did Bobby Charlton score for England?
    a) 47
    b) 48
    c) 49

20. In what year did England take part in their first World Cup?
    a) 1930
    b) 1950
    c) 1966

Answers to Quiz 5: Pot Luck

1. Stoke City
2. Sheffield United
3. Jose Mourinho
4. Lazio
5. Tottenham Hotspur
6. Arsene Wenger
7. True
8. Thierry Henry
9. Tottenham Hotspur
10. Genoa
11. Crystal Palace
12. Gianfranco Zola
13. Newcastle United
14. Chris Powell
15. Bayern Munich
16. Kevin Keegan
17. Bobby Moore
18. Crystal Palace, Plymouth Argyle, Port Vale, Rochdale, Morecambe and Dagenham & Redbridge
19. Holland
20. Easter Road

EASY

Quiz 7: Pot Luck

1. Who, in 2012, became the first midfielder to score 150 Premier League goals?

2. Which two players missed penalties in England's 1990 World Cup semifinal against West Germany?

3. Who played Brian Clough in the 2009 film The Damned United?

4. What country will host the 2022 World Cup?

5. What is Edson Arantes Do Nascimento more commonly known as?

6. Who is the only foreigner to manage the Scotland national team?

7. Which manager gave Hull City's players a half-time dressing down on the pitch in 2008?

8. Which family bought Manchester United in 2005?

9. Keep Right On To The End Of The Road is sung by supporters of which team?

10. Which Irishman holds the record for the most appearances by an Arsenal player?

11. Which TV pundit famously said, 'You'll never win anything with kids'?

12. Which Premier League goalkeeper went 1,311 minutes without conceding a goal in 2008/09?

13. Steven Fry is a fan of which club?

14. Who succeeded Bill Shankly as Liverpool manager?

15. Which English team is nicknamed The Tractor Boys?

16. Who was the first Brazilian to play in English football?

17. Who did Stoke City beat to win the League Cup in 1972?

18. Who comes next on this list – Alan Curbishley, Gianfranco Zola, Avram Grant?

19. QPR's mercurial midfielder Adel Taraabt is an international for which country?
    a) Algeria
    b) France
    c) Morocco

20. All of Spain's goals at the 2010 World Cup were scored by players from which club?
    A) Barcelona
    b) Real Madrid
    c) Valencia

Answers to Quiz 6: England

1. Geoff Hurst (3) and Martin Peters
2. Theo Walcott
3. Cameroon
4. Shearer (2) and Sheringham (2)
5. Bobby Robson
6. Michael Owen (3), Steven Gerrard and Emile Heskey
7. Stanley Matthews
8. Viv Anderson
9. Gareth Southgate
10. Germany 4-1
11. None
12. Peter Crouch
13. Brazil
14. Scotland
15. Steve McClaren
16. Gary and Phil Neville
17. Alf Ramsey
18. Peter Shilton
19. 49
20. 1950

EASY

15

Quiz 8: World Cup

EASY

1. Which two countries were the first to co-host a World Cup?

2. Which country won the first World Cup?

3. Which Barcelona player scored the winning goal in the 2010 World Cup final?

4. What is the only country to have taken part in every World Cup to date?

5. Who was the England manager at the 1982 World Cup?

6. In what year did the Republic of Ireland reach the World Cup finals for the first time?

7. Who were the first country to win the World Cup after a penalty shoot-out?

8. What is the only country to reach three World Cup finals and lose every one?

9. Which cricket legend played in World Cup qualifiers for Antigua and Barbuda in 1974?

10. Which country will host the 2014 World Cup?

11. Which midfielder was the only player to score more than one goal for England at the 2006 World Cup finals?

12. Who is the only Englishman to be the top scorer at a World Cup?

13. Which country reached the World Cup final in 1982, 1986 and 1990?

14. Zinedine Zidane was sent off in the 2006 final after head-butting which Italian defender?

15. The 1982 World Cup was held in which country?

16. Which country reached the semifinal of the 1998 World Cup but didn't qualify for the 2002 tournament?

17. How many teams took part in the 2010 World Cup?

18. In what year was the first World Cup held?

19. Which team drew 1-1 with Italy in the 2010 World Cup?
    a) Australia
    b) New Zealand
    c) North Korea

20. The first World Cup was held in which country?
    a) Brazil
    b) France
    c) Uruguay

EASY

Answers to Quiz 7: Pot Luck

1. Frank Lampard
2. Chris Waddle and Stuart Pearce
3. Michael Sheen
4. Qatar
5. Pele
6. Berti Vogts
7. Phil Brown
8. The Glazers
9. Birmingham City
10. David O'Leary
11. Alan Hansen
12. Edwin van der Sar
13. Norwich City
14. Bob Paisley
15. Ipswich Town
16. Mirandinha
17. Chelsea
18. Sam Allardyce
19. Morocco
20. Barcelona

Quiz 9: Pot Luck

1. Which club was the first in England to have an all-seater stadium?

2. Filbert Street was the former home of which club?

3. Who holds the record for the most appearances by a Manchester United player?

4. Which former England captain insisted on being the last player out of the dressing room and always put his shirt on as he ran onto the pitch?

5. Which club's supporters regularly go 'boing, boing'?

6. Burnley and Bolton manager Owen Coyle briefly played international football for which country?

7. The much-travelled Nicolas Anelka had spells at which five Premier League clubs?

8. The Trotters is the nickname of which English club?

9. Which Premier League club is known as the School of Science?

10. Which former department store owner took over Fulham in 1997?

11. Who was the last player playing in the third tier of English football to win a full England cap?

12. Which English Football League club contains the letters A, B, C, D and E?

13. Who did Kenny Dalglish succeed as manager on his return to Anfield in 2011?

14. In 2010, Raul left Real Madrid to join which German club?

15. Who was known as the Baby-Faced Assassin?

16. Which club has won the most Spanish league titles?

17. Who is the only player to play first teams games for Manchester United, Manchester City, Everton and Liverpool?

18. What is the only Football League club that doesn't contain any of the letters from the word mackerel in its name?

19. Who did Liverpool beat in the 2012 FA Cup semifinal?
    a) Everton
    b) Cardiff
    c) Manchester City

20. Who is Manchester United's all-time leading league goalscorer?
    a) Bobby Charlton
    b) Denis Law
    c) Wayne Rooney

Answers to Quiz 8: World Cup

1.	Japan and South Korea	11.	Steven Gerrard
2.	Uruguay	12.	Gary Lineker in 1986
3.	Andrés Iniesta	13.	West Germany
4.	Brazil	14.	Marco Materazzi
5.	Ron Greenwood	15.	Spain
6.	1990	16.	Holland
7.	Brazil in 1994	17.	32
8.	Holland	18.	1930
9.	Viv Richards	19.	New Zealand
10.	Brazil	20.	Uruguay

Quiz 10: Champions League/ European Cup

1. Who, in 1967, became the first British winners of the European Cup?

2. Who did Manchester United beat in their maiden 1968 triumph?

3. Which team won the first five European Cup finals?

4. Who scored five goals against Bayer Leverkusen in 2012?

5. Who were the first team to win the trophy when it became the Champions League?

6. Manchester United completed their famous 1999 treble by beating which team in the Champions League final?

7. Who were the first team from Eastern Europe to win the European Cup?

8. Which English club lost in their only European Cup final appearance in 1975?

9. Which city was the venue for Liverpool's 2005 triumph over AC Milan?

10. In the late 1970s and early 1980s, English teams claimed the trophy for how many successive seasons?

11. Which German missed the crucial shoot-out spot kick in the 2012 Champions League final?

12. Which city hosted the 2008 final between Manchester United and Chelsea?

13. Who scored for Chelsea in their 2-2 draw at Barcelona in the 2012 Champions League semifinal?

14. Which German club did Liverpool beat to win their first European Cup?

15. Which brothers played in both the 1995 and 1996 Champions League final?

16. Which three Dutch clubs have been champions of Europe?

17. Who were the only team to beat Barcelona in the 2010/11 Champions League season?

18. Which two clubs that have appeared in at least two finals have a 100% record?

19. Who did Barcelona beat in the 2011 final?
    a) Arsenal
    b) Chelsea
    c) Manchester United

20. Which Arsenal player was the first man to be sent off in a Champions League final?
    a) Sol Campbell
    b) Denis Bergkamp
    c) Jens Lehmann

EASY

Answers to Quiz 9: Pot Luck

1. Coventry City
2. Leicester City
3. Ryan Giggs
4. Paul Ince
5. West Bromwich Albion's
6. Republic of Ireland
7. Arsenal, Liverpool, Manchester City, Bolton and Chelsea
8. Bolton Wanderers
9. Everton
10. Mohammed Al Fayed

11. Steve Bull
12. Wycombe Wanderers (in the Conference, Cambridge United do too)
13. Roy Hodgson
14. Schalke 04
15. Ole Gunnar Solskjaer
16. Real Madrid
17. Peter Beardsley
18. Swindon Town
19. Everton
20. Bobby Charlton

Quiz 11: Pot Luck

1. What is the only team in Europe to have won the European Cup more often than their domestic league championship?

2. Who were the first club in England to install an artificial pitch?

3. While exiled from The Valley, Charlton shared a ground with which two clubs?

4. Bobby Moore is most commonly associated with West Ham but he also played for what other English club?

5. Which Italian took over as Swindon Town boss in 2011?

6. Robbie Keane enjoyed a spell on loan at Aston Villa from which American team?

7. Which Blackburn goalkeeper was deceived by a divot to gift Stan Collymore a goal in 1996?

8. Which French international kissed Fabien Barthez's bald head before every game?

9. The Blaydon Races is a song associated with which club?

10. Who scored eight goals in a 12-game loan spell with Bolton Wanderers in 2011?

11. Who was the first player in the world to win a century of international caps?

12. Former England captain and now Radio 5 pundit Jimmy Armfield spent all of his playing career with which club?

13. London Road is the home ground of which club?

14. Which father and son made over 850 appearances for West Ham?

15. Who was sacked as Huddersfield Town manager in February 2012 despite the club losing only three of their previous 55 games?

EASY

16. Which club lost in the final of both the FA Cup and League Cup in 1993?

17. Who saved three penalties in the 2006 FA Cup final shoot-out between Liverpool and West Ham?

18. What is the South American equivalent of the European Championships?

19. Who were the last team other than Real Madrid or Barcelona to win the Spanish title?
a) Atletico Madrid
b) Sevilla
c) Valencia

20. How many teams took part in the first Premier League season?
a) 20
b) 22
c) 24

Answers to Quiz 10: Champions League/European Cup

1. Celtic
2. Benfica
3. Real Madrid
4. Lionel Messi
5. Marseille
6. Bayern Munich
7. Steaua Bucharest
8. Leeds United
9. Istanbul
10. Six
11. Bastian Schweinsteiger
12. Moscow
13. Ramires and Torres
14. Borussia Mönchengladbach
15. Frank and Ronald de Boer
16. Ajax, Feyenoord and PSV Eindhoven
17. Arsenal
18. Nottingham Forest and Porto
19. Manchester United
20. Jens Lehmann

Quiz 12: European Championship

1. Which two countries hosted Euro 2012?

2. Who was the top scorer at Euro 96?

3. In what year did a Ruud Gullit-inspired Dutch team win the Euros?

4. Which Spanish striker scored the only goal in his country's 1-0 win over Germany in the 2008 final?

5. What country won Euro 92 despite not originally qualifying for the tournament?

6. Who famously sat in 'the dentist's chair' after scoring a spectacular goal at Euro 96?

7. France won the competition in 1984. Who did they beat in the final?

8. David Seaman saved whose penalty in England's 2-0 win over Scotland in Euro 96?

9. Who were the first European Champions who went on to win the World Cup two years later?

10. England failed to qualify in 2008 after losing their final qualification game against which country?

11. When was the last time Scotland qualified for the European Championships?

12. Ireland booked their place at Euro 2012 after winning a play-off against which former Soviet republic?

13. Which striker wore the number 9 shirt for England at Euro 2012?

14. Who did England play in their opening match at Euro 2012?

15. Which two countries hosted Euro 2008?

16. In 1980, which country became the first to win the European Championships twice?

17. Which Birmingham goalkeeper, who spent most of the 2011/12 season on loan at Cheltenham, was a member of England's Euro 2012 aquad?

18. Who scored a brilliant hat trick against England in the 1988 finals?

19. Which team was not drawn in England's group at Euro 2012?
    a) Russia
    b) Sweden
    c) Ukraine

20. In what year did the first European Championships take place?
    a) 1952
    b) 1956
    c) 1960

Answers to Quiz 11: Pot Luck

1. Nottingham Forest
2. QPR
3. Crystal Palace and West Ham
4. Fulham
5. Paolo di Canio
6. LA Galaxy
7. Tim Flowers
8. Laurent Blanc
9. Newcastle United
10. Daniel Sturridge
11. Billy Wright
12. Blackpool
13. Peterborough United
14. Frank Lampard Sr and Jr
15. Lee Clark
16. Sheffield Wednesday
17. Pepe Reina
18. Copa America
19. Valencia
20. 22

Quiz 13: Pot Luck

EASY

1. Which team's mascot became an elected mayor in 2002?

2. Which former World Footballer of the year was defeated in the 2005 presidential election in Liberia?

3. The Chuckle Brothers are honorary presidents of which club?

4. Manchester United signed defender Patrice Evra from which French club?

5. Who succeeded Kenny Dalglish as Liverpool manager in 1991?

6. Who is the only Englishman to win the Premier League Manager of the Season award?

7. Which club in the top four divisions in England has the shortest name?

8. Who succeeded Alex McLeish as manager of Birmingham City?

9. Which Bolton player suffered a heart attack during his side's FA Cup tie against Spurs in 2012?

10. Actors Keith Allen and Hugh Grant are followers of which London team?

11. Since 1974, the classified football results on the BBC's Sports Report have been read by which legendary broadcaster?

12. What is the piece of music 'Drum Majorette' by Barry Stroller more commonly known as?

13. Manchester City's Etihad Stadium was originally built for which event?

14. At which ground will you find the Gallowgate End?

15. Who did Pep Guardiola succeed as manager of Barcelona?

16. 'For the Game. For the World' is the motto of which organisation?

17. Arsenal legend Dennis Bergkamp joined the Gunners from which club?

18. Which brainy footballer has 11 GCSEs, including, famously an A* in Latin?

19. Who is Liverpool's all-time leading goal scorer?
    a) John Aldridge
    b) Kenny Dalglish
    c) Ian Rush

20. Midfielder Aaron Ramsey made his professional debut for which club?
    a) Cardiff City
    b) Swansea City
    c) Arsenal

Answers to Quiz 12: European Championship

1. Poland and Ukraine	11. 1996
2. Alan Shearer	12. Estonia
3. 1988	13. Andy Carroll
4. Fernando Torres	14. France
5. Denmark	15. Austria and Switzerland
6. Paul Gascoigne	16. West Germany
7. Spain	17. Jack Buckland
8. Gary McAllister	18. Marco Van Basten
9. West Germany	19. Russia
10. Croatia	20. 1960

Quiz 14: Nicknames part 1

Can you identify which clubs have the following nicknames?

1. The Bantams

2. The Clarets

3. The Hornets

4. The Baggies

5. The Brewers

6. The Grecians

7. The Eagles

8. The Cherries

9. The Iron

10. The Millers

11. The Blades

12. The Posh

13. The Chairboys

14. The Railwaymen

15. The Addicks

16. The Seasiders

17. The Shakers

18. The Shrimpers

19. The Terriers

20. The Owls

Answers to Quiz 13: Pot Luck

1. Hartlepool United
2. George Weah
3. Rotherham United
4. Monaco
5. Graeme Souness
6. Harry Redknapp
7. Bury
8. Chris Hughton
9. Fabrice Muamba
10. Fulham
11. James Alexander Gordon

12. The theme music to Match of the Day
13. 2002 Commonwealth Games
14. Newcastle's St James' Park
15. Frank Rijkaard
16. FIFA
17. Internazionale
18. Frank Lampard
19. John Aldridge
20. Cardiff City

Quiz 15: Pot Luck

1. In what sport have strikers Mick Channon and Mick Quinn gone on to enjoy success?

2. Which journalist is the host of Sky TV's Sunday Supplement?

3. Snooker, darts and boxing promoter Barry Hearn is the chairman of which club?

4. How did Charlton's Keith Peacock make history in 1965?

5. Former prime minister Tony Blair is a fan of which football club?

6. Blue Is The Colour was was a top 5 hit for the players of which club?

7. Who scored all four goals in Arsenal's 4-4 draw with Liverpool at Anfield in April 2009?

8. Which Frenchman stepped down as Aston Villa manager in 2011?

9. What name comes next on this list – Tony Parkes, Graeme Souness, Mark Hughes?

10. Who did Owen Coyle succeed as manager of Bolton Wanderers?

11. Which tough-tackling Chelsea defender was nicknamed Chopper?

12. Which club's nickname is thought to have derived from a sweet shop called Mother Noblett's?

13. Who was Arsenal's last permanent manager before Arsene Wenger took over in 1996?

14. Which country qualified for the 1950 World Cup but withdrew as some of their players wanted to play barefoot?

15. Which two teams have lost the most World Cup penalty shoot-outs?

16. Who are the three Dutch players to have been named European Footballer of the Year?

17. Which manager avoided a driving ban after his lawyer argued that it would have caused hardship to the people of the town in which he managed?

18. Which French player was sent home from the 2010 World Cup after a row with his manager?

19. Fernando Torres joined Liverpool from which club?
    a) Atletico Madrid
    b) Athletic Bilbao
    c) Real Madrid

20. Which full-time England manager had the shortest reign?
    a) Steve McClaren
    b) Don Revie
    c) Terry Venables

Answers to Quiz 14: Nicknames

1. Bradford City
2. Burnley
3. Watford
4. West Bromwich Albion
5. Burton Albion
6. Exeter City
7. Crystal Palace
8. Bournemouth
9. Scunthorpe United
10. Rotherham United
11. Sheffield United
12. Peterborough United
13. Wycombe Wanderers
14. Crewe Alexandra
15. Charlton Athletic
16. Blackpool
17. Bury
18. Southend United
19. Huddersfield Town
20. Sheffield Wednesday

Quiz 16: Midfield Maestros

1. Who came out of retirement to help Manchester United's title challenge in 2012?

2. Which Arsenal and England midfielder missed the whole of the 2011/12 season due to injury?

3. David Silva joined Manchester City from which Spanish club?

4. Who is England's most capped midfielder?

5. Manchester United and England winger Ashley Young made his league debut for which club?

6. Which Dutch legend ended his career at Crystal Palace in 2010?

7. Who was known as Captain Marvel?

8. Which battling midfielder won the 2011 Football Writers' Association Player of the Year award?

9. Which English midfielder was runner-up in the FIFA World Player of the Year award voting in 2005?

10. Which midfielder scored a last-minute winner for England against Belgium in the 1990 World Cup?

11. Yaya Toure plays his international football for which country?

12. Which midfielder was England's captain at the 2010 World Cup?

13. Which Hungarian midfielder started his Premier League career at West Brom, joined Fulham, then returned to Albion in 2011?

14. Which Blackburn and Birmingham midfielder won his only cap against Portugal in 2002?

15. Who started his career with Cannes, had a brief spell with Milan, spent nine years in the Premier League, headed back to Italy for five years before finishing his career in England?

16. Roy Keane ended his playing career at which club?

EASY

17. Which Croatian club did Luka Modric play for before joining Spurs in 2008?

18. Which Manchester United midfielder was forced to take a break from football in 2011 after being diagnosed with ulcerative colitis?

19. England international Owen Hargreaves was born in which country?
a) Canada
b) Germany
c) USA

20. Which battling midfielder damaged ankle ligaments when his three-year-old daughter ran over his foot while riding her tricycle?
a) David Batty
b) Paul Ince
c) Roy Keane

Answers to Quiz 15: Pot Luck

1. Horse racing
2. Brian Woolnough
3. Leyton Orient
4. He was the first substitute in a Football League game
5. Newcastle United
6. Chelsea
7. Andrei Arshavin
8. Gérard Houllier
9. Paul Ince (Blackburn Rovers managers)
10. Gary Megson
11. Ron Harris
12. Everton (The Toffeemen)
13. Bruce Rioch
14. India
15. England and Italy
16. Johann Cruyff, Ruud Gullit and Marco van Basten
17. Tony Pulis
18. Nicolas Anelka
19. Atletico Madrid
20. Steve McClaren

Quiz 17: Pot Luck

1. Chef Delia Smith is associated with which football club?

2. Which English football club has the Latin motto nil satis nisi optimum?

3. Which legendary German footballer was known as Der Kaiser?

4. Arsenal midfielder Jack Wilshere spent part of the 2009/10 season on loan at which club?

5. England's players collaborated with which group for the 1990 anthem World In Motion?

6. True or false – Anfield legend Jamie Carragher was a childhood supporter of Everton?

7. Manchester City fans borrowed their back-turning celebration from which Polish club?

8. What word connects a political party launched by George Galloway and an FA campaign launched in 2008 to improve the behaviour of players and coaches towards referees?

9. Which rugged central defender received his ninth Premier League red card against Wigan in January 2009?

10. Craig Bellamy made his English league debut for which club?

11. Tim Cahill joined Everton from which club?

12. Which former Crewe, Norwich and West Ham forward was forced to retire from the game in 2009, aged just 26?

13. David Beckham famously scored for Manchester United with a shot from his own half in 1996. Who were United's opponents that day?

14. Which England international scored after just 7 seconds for Hull City against Walsall in 2004?

15. What is the name of the Indian company that took over Blackburn Rovers in 2010?

16. Which England forward was nicknamed the Lion of Vienna?

17. What is the only Football League club whose name contains no letters that can be coloured in?

18. Which team overturned a 4-0 deficit at half time to secure an unlikely draw against Arsenal in February 2011?

19. In terms of trophies won, who is Liverpool's most successful manager?
    a) Bill Shankly
    b) Bob Paisley
    c) Rafa Benitez

20. Which action star famously watched Everton in a Premier League game in 2007?
    a) Arnold Schwarzenegger
    b) Sylvester Stallone
    c) Bruce Willis

EASY

Answers to Quiz 16: Midfield Maestros

1.	Paul Scholes	11.	Ivory Coast
2.	Jack Wilshere	12.	Steven Gerrard
3.	Valencia	13.	Zoltan Gera
4.	David Beckham	14.	David Dunn
5.	Watford	15.	Patrick Vieira
6.	Edgar Davids	16.	Celtic
7.	Bryan Robson	17.	Dynamo Zagreb
8.	Scott Parker	18.	Darren Fletcher
9.	Frank Lampard	19.	Canada
10.	David Platt	20.	David Batty

Quiz 18: Quote, Unquote

Identify the people who said the following quotes:

1. 'Some people believe football is a matter of life and death. I'm very disappointed with that attitude. I can assure you it is much, much more important than that.'

2. 'I wouldn't say I was the best manager in the business. But I was in the top one.'

3. 'When the seagulls follow the trawler, it is because they think sardines will be thrown into the sea.'

4. 'It's a huge honour to wear No 7 at Liverpool. I think about the legends: Dalglish, Keegan and that Australian guy.'

5. 'It was a very simple team talk. All I used to say was: 'Whenever possible, give the ball to George Best.'

6. 'There's only two types of manager. Those who've been sacked and those who will be sacked in the future.'

7. 'There is no pressure at the top. The pressure is being second or third.'

8. 'The game is about glory, it is about doing things in style and with a flourish.'

9. 'Football is simple but the hardest thing to do is play simple football.'

10. 'Football and cookery are the two most important subjects in the country.'

11. 'I was, I am and I always will be a drug addict. A person who gets involved in drugs has to fight it every day.'

12. 'Can you believe that? A female linesman ... women don't know the offside rule.'

13. 'There is no chance I would ever consider having all my hair cut off. My hair is my life. If you cut off my hair, it is like cutting out my heart. I would cry for days and days.'

14. 'There is nothing to do in Manchester.'

15. 'Rome wasn't built in a day, but I wasn't on that particular job.'

16. 'I was upset. In 2011 you can't say things like this. He knows what he said, the ref knows. It will come out.'

17. 'I am the best. I don't need a Ballon d'Or to prove I am No. 1.'

18. 'It was our worst-ever day, the worst result in my history, ever. Even as a player I don't think I ever lost 6-1.'

19. 'Sitting eating sushi in the city, incredibly chilled out reading Nietzsche.'

20. 'Just to confirm to all my followers I have had a hair transplant. I was going bald at 25, why not?'

Answers to Quiz 17: Pot Luck

1. Norwich City
2. Everton
3. Franz Beckenbauer
4. Bolton Wanderers
5. New Order
6. True
7. Lech Poznan
8. Respect
9. Richard Dunne
10. Norwich City
11. Millwall
12. Dean Ashton
13. Wimbledon
14. Nick Barmby
15. Venky
16. Nat Lofthouse
17. Hull City
18. Newcastle United
19. Bob Paisley
20. Sylvester Stallone

Quiz 19: Pot Luck

1. Who were briefly joint managers of Liverpool in 1998?

2. Which former England captain presented the trophy at the 2012 FA Cup final?

3. Sol Campbell played one game for which League 2 club in 2009?

4. Cricket legend Ian Botham played 11 games for which Football League club?

5. In what year did the Munich air crash happen?

6. Which Premier League team were 'Invincible' in 2003/04?

7. Which manager was nicknamed The Tinker Man?

8. Who holds the record for the most appearances by an Everton player?

9. How often does the Africa Cup of Nations take place?

10. True or false – Argentina fans created a religion called Iglesia Maradoniana in honour of the Hand of God-inspired striker?

11. Who uttered the famous line, 'Some people are on the pitch. They think it's all over...it is now'?

12. In which country do teams compete for the Scudetto?

13. Audere est facere is the Latin motto of which Premier League club?

14. What are the eight English cities that can host derby matches?

15. Who resigned as Aston Villa manager five days before the start of the 2010/11 season?

16. They Think It's All Over host Nick Hancock is a fan of which club?

17. Who did Laurent Blanc succeed as manager of the French national team?

18. What nationality is Chelsea midfielder Ramires?

19. Boca Juniors are one of the biggest clubs in which country?
    a) Argentina
    b) Brazil
    c) Uruguay

20. Who steered Sheffield Wednesday to promotion from League One in 2012?
    a) Micky Adams
    b) Dave Jones
    c) Gary Megson

Answers to Quiz 18: Quote, Unquote

1. Bill Shankly
2. Brian Clough
3. Eric Cantona
4. Luis Suarez
5. Matt Busby
6. Howard Wilkinson
7. Jose Mourinho
8. Danny Blanchflower
9. Johan Cruyff
10. Delia Smith
11. Diego Maradona
12. Andy Gray
13. Anderson
14. Carlos Tevez
15. Brian Clough
16. Patrice Evra
17. Zlatan Ibrahimovic
18. Alex Ferguson
19. Joey Barton
20. Wayne Rooney

Quiz 20: Scottish Football

1. Which team has won the most top-flight Scottish League titles?

2. Who did Celtic beat in the 1967 European Cup final?

3. Dens Park is the home ground of which club?

4. Which teams met in the 2012 Scottish Cup final?

5. Which Scottish club play their home games at Hampden Park?

6. Who are the two foreigners to have managed Rangers?

7. What is the only Scottish team to have won two European trophies?

8. Up to and including 2012, which team had won the most Scottish Cups?

9. Who did Rangers beat in the 1972 European Cup Winners' Cup final?

10. What is the name of Motherwell's home ground?

11. Who is the only Spaniard to get on the scoresheet for the winning team in a Scottish Cup final?

12. What was the venue for Rangers' Uefa Cup final defeat against Zenit St Petersburg in 2008?

13. Which Englishman, whose surname is a capital city, made 11 appearances for Celtic in 2006?

14. Who holds the record for the most appearances for Celtic?

15. The record win in British football history was 36-0. Who won and who did they beat?

16. The Bairns is the nickname of which club?

17. Celtic have had two English managers. Can you name them?

18. Which two Celtic players share the record for the most goals in an SPL season?

19. Which club won their only SPL title in 1982/83?
    a) Aberdeen
    b) Dundee
    c) Dundee United

20. How many league titles did Rangers win under Walter Smith?
    a) 9
    b) 10
    c) 11

EASY

Answers to Quiz 19: Pot Luck

1. Roy Evans and Gérard Houllier
2. Jimmy Armfield
3. Notts County
4. Scunthorpe United
5. 1958
6. Arsenal
7. Claudio Ranieri
8. Neville Southall
9. Every 2 years
10. True
11. Kenneth Wolstenholme
12. Italy
13. Tottenham Hotspur
14. London, Birmingham, Manchester, Liverpool, Stoke, Sheffield, Nottingham, Bristol
15. Martin O'Neill
16. Stoke City
17. Raymond Domenech
18. Brazilian
19. Argentina
20. Dave Jones

Quiz 21: Pot Luck

1. Who did Chelsea beat in the 2010 FA Cup final?

2. Everton's Nikica Jelavic plays international football for which country?

3. Which manager led Lazio to only their second Serie A title in 2000?

4. Prolific poacher Darren Bent joined Aston Villa from which club?

5. Who did Sam Allardyce succeed as manager of Blackburn Rovers?

6. Martin O'Neill steered which Conference club into the Football League for the first time in 1993?

7. Which team lost penalty shoot-outs at Euro 92, Euro 96, World Cup 98 and Euro 2000?

8. The final of Euro 2012 was hosted in which city?

9. In which city will you find the clubs Vasco de Gama, Flamengo and Fluminese?

10. Who was the first player to score 100 Premier League goals?

11. Which Italian club is known as the 'Grand Old Lady'?

12. Who was the first African player to be named FIFA World Player of the Year?

13. Dreamboat is the nickname of which Newcastle midfielder?

14. Which prolific goalscorer said of his move to Juventus, 'I couldn't settle in Italy – it was like living in a foreign country'?

15. Mario Balotelli joined Manchester City from which Italian club?

16. Which manager steered Reading to promotion to the Premier League in 2012?

17. Oakwell is the home ground of which English club?

18. Which Premier League-winning strike pairing was nicknamed the SAS?

19. Which team won their first nine games at the start of the 2005/06 Premier League season?
a) Arsenal
b) Chelsea
c) Manchester United

20. Which country won their first Africa Cup of Nations title in 2012?
a) Botswana
b) Zambia
c) Zimbabwe

Answers to Quiz 20: Scottish Football

1. Rangers
2. Inter Milan
3. Dundee
4. Hearts and Hibernian
5. Queen's Park
6. Dick Advocaat and Paul Le Guen
7. Aberdeen (Cup Winners' Cup and European Super Cup)
8. Celtic
9. Barcelona
10. Fir Park
11. Nacho Novo
12. City of Manchester Stadium
13. Dion Dublin
14. Billy McNeill
15. Arbroath beat Bon Accord
16. Falkirk
17. John Barnes and Tony Mowbray
18. Henrik Larsson and Brian McClair with 35
19. Dundee United
20. 10

Quiz 22: Wales

1. Who is Wales' most capped goalkeeper?

2. Wales' biggest ever win, 11-0, came against which country?

3. Wales made their only appearance in the World Cup finals in what year?

4. Who was the first player to score for Wales at the Millennium Stadium?

5. With 28 goals in 73 games, who is Wales' all-time leading goal scorer?

6. Who is the youngest player ever to play for Wales?

7. Who missed a penalty in Wales' crucial World Cup qualifier against Romania in Cardiff in 1993?

8. Wales played a memorial match in honour of Gary Speed against which Central American country?

9. How many times have Wales qualified for the European Championships?

10. Aged just 20, who became Wales' youngest captain in 2011?

11. Who are the two English-born managers to have taken charge of the Welsh national team?

12. Which of the home nations is in the same World Cup 2014 qualification group as Wales?

13. Which Welsh legend was nicknamed 'The Gentle Giant'?

14. Who scored a hat trick for Wales in their 4-0 demolition of Scotland at the Millennium Stadium in 2004?

15. Who were the first team to play Wales at the Millennium Stadium?

16. Which team beat Wales in a play-off to qualify for the 2004 European Championships?

17. Who succeeded Mark Hughes as manager of the Welsh team?

18. Wales famously thrashed England 4-1 in 1980 at which ground?

19. Which team eliminated Wales in their only World Cup appearance to date?
    a) Argentina
    b) Brazil
    c) Uruguay

20. How far did they get in the competition?
    a) first round
    b) quarterfinal
    c) semifinal

Answers to Quiz 21: Pot Luck

1. Portsmouth
2. Croatia
3. Sven Goran Eriksson
4. Sunderland
5. Paul Ince
6. Wycombe Wanderers
7. Holland
8. Kiev
9. Rio de Janeiro
10. Alan Shearer
11. Juventus
12. George Weah
13. Yohan Cabaye
14. Ian Rush
15. Internazionale
16. Brian McDermott
17. Barnsley
18. Chris Sutton and Alan Shearer
19. Chelsea
20. Zambia

Quiz 23: Pot Luck

1. Who did Paul Jewell succeed as Ipswich manager in 2011?

2. Which Irish international scored 329 league goals for Newport, Oxford, Liverpool and Tranmere?

3. Alan Shearer got his first start in league football for which club?

4. Who wrote the classic football book Fever Pitch?

5. 'Mes que un club' is the motto of which European giant?

6. Manchester City skipper Vincent Kompany plays his international football for which country?

7. What sort of kit did Birkenhead rockers Half Man Half Biscuit want for Christmas?

8. Which legendary striker was nicknamed 'The Galloping Major'?

9. Which Premier League ground shares its name with the site of an 11th-century battle?

10. Which Scot was the oldest player to take part in the 2012 European Championship qualifiers?

11. Who is the only Liverpool-born player to score a hat trick for Liverpool in a Merseyside derby?

12. Who were the only team to break the 100-point barrier in the 2011/12 Football League season?

13. Who finished runners-up behind Celtic in the SPL in 2012?

14. Who did Liverpool beat in the 2012 Carling Cup final?

15. Kenny Dalglish has managed which four clubs?

EASY

16. Which two countries beginning with the letter S qualified for Euro 2012?

17. Who was the first player-manager to lead his side to the top division title?

18. Manchester United's greatest ever victory was a 10-0 win over which Belgian team?

19. Stade Velodrome is the home ground of which French club?
    a) Bordeaux
    b) Lyon
    c) Marseille

20. Which event was held first?
    a) Africa Cup of Nations
    b) European Championships

Answers to Quiz 22: Wales

1. Neville Southall
2. Ireland
3. 1958
4. Ryan Giggs
5. Ian Rush
6. Gareth Bale
7. Paul Bodin
8. Costa Rica
9. Never
10. Aaron Ramsey
11. Mike Smith and Bobby Gould
12. Scotland
13. John Charles
14. Robert Earnshaw
15. Finland
16. Russia
17. John Toshack
18. Wrexham's Racecourse Ground
19. Brazil
20. Quarterfinal

Quiz 24: Northern Ireland

EASY

1. Northern Ireland play their home games at which ground?

2. Michael O'Neill, who was appointed manager of Northern Ireland in 2011, was formerly manager of which club?

3. Who is Northern Ireland's most capped player?

4. Who played and managed Northern Ireland in World Cup finals?

5. How many times have Northern Ireland qualified for the World Cup finals?

6. David Healy scored a hat trick in a shock 3-2 win over which country in September 2006?

7. Who made his 88th and final appearance for Northern Ireland against Italy in October 2011?

8. Who scored the only goal in Northern Ireland's famous win over England in 2005?

9. How many caps did George Best win with Northern Ireland?

10. Who captained Northern Ireland in the 1958 World Cup?

11. During Sammy McIlroy's reign, Northern Ireland went how many games without scoring a goal?

12. True or false – Northern Ireland were the last winners of the British Home Championship?

13. How many times have Northern Ireland qualified for the European Championships?

14. Who are Northern Ireland's two English-born managers?

15. Who scored the only goal in Northern Ireland's 1-0 win over hosts Spain in the 1982 World Cup?

16. Who succeeded Lawrie Sanchez as Northern Ireland manager?

17. Who is Northern Ireland's all-time leading international goalscorer?

18. Who was the first black player to play for Northern Ireland?

19. Which of the following aren't in Northern Ireland's 2014 World Cup qualifying group?
a) Portugal
b) Russia
c) Spain

20. What is the highest position Northern Ireland have reached in the FIFA World Rankings?
a) 27
b) 37
c) 47

Answers to Quiz 23: Pot Luck

1. Roy Keane
2. John Aldridge
3. Southampton
4. Nick Hornby
5. Barcelona
6. Belgium
7. A Dukla Prague away kit
8. Ferenc Puskas
9. Stamford Bridge
10. David Weir
11. Steven Gerrard
12. Charlton Athletic
13. Motherwell
14. Cardiff
15. Liverpool, Blackburn, Newcastle and Celtic
16. Spain and Sweden
17. Kenny Dalglish
18. Anderlecht
19. Marseille
20. Africa Cup of Nations

Quiz 25: Pot Luck

EASY

1. Which African country's national team are nicknamed The Indomitable Lions?

2. Which country won the first Olympic football gold medal in 1908?

3. Who was the first player sold for a £1m transfer fee?

4. Which Football League club are nicknamed The Tigers?

5. What animal features on the Chelsea badge?

6. Who scored five times in Manchester United's 7-1 win over Blackburn in 2010?

7. Alex McLeish left which club to take over at Aston Villa?

8. The Boleyn Ground is the home of which London club?

9. What was the name of the mascot of the 1966 World Cup?

10. Which Scottish club call Tynecastle home?

11. Who succeeded Andre Villas Boas as Chelsea manager?

12. Which manager said on winning promotion to the Premier League in 2010, 'I couldn't be more chuffed if I were a badger at the start of the mating season'?

13. The name of which Spanish club translates into English as Royal Society?

14. The son of which dictator had spells in Italian football at Perugia, Udinese and Sampdoria?

15. What nickname is shared by Luton Town and Stockport County?

16. Who was the youngest player in England's 1966 World Cup winning team?

17. How many times have Tottenham won England's top flight?

18. What two English cities have each produced two Premier League champions?

19. What is Manchester United's lowest league finish since the Premier League began?
    a) 2nd
    b) 3rd
    c) 4th

20. Which Italian club does not wear blue and black stripes?
    a) Atalanta
    b) Internazionale
    c) Genoa

Answers to Quiz 24: Northern Ireland

1. Windsor Park
2. Shamrock Rovers
3. Pat Jennings
4. Billy Bingham
5. Three times
6. Spain
7. Maik Taylor
8. David Healy
9. 37
10. Danny Blanchflower
11. 10
12. True
13. Never
14. Lawrie McMenemy and Lawrie Sanchez
15. Gerry Armstrong
16. Nigel Worthington
17. David Healy
18. Jeff Whitley
19. Spain
20. 27

Quiz 26: Republic of Ireland

1. In what year did Ireland first qualify for the European Championships?

2. Who was the first Irishman to make 100 appearances for the national side?

3. Who walked out on the squad at the 2002 World Cup after a row with Mick McCarthy?

4. Ireland qualified for the 2002 World Cup after winning a play-off against which country?

5. Who did the Irish famously beat in their first European Championship appearance?

6. Which country did Ireland beat in their opening match of the 1994 World Cup?

7. Who is the Republic's all-time leading goalscorer?

8. Which player-manager led Ireland between 1973 and 1980?

9. Which midfielder scored Ireland's first ever goal in the World Cup finals?

10. Who played in 66 consecutive competitive internationals for Ireland between 1999 and 2011?

11. Ireland lost on penalties to which team in the 2002 World Cup?

12. The first game at the Aviva Stadium saw Ireland take on which South American side?

13. Who is Ireland's most capped goalkeeper?

14. Giovanni Trapattoni left which club to take the Ireland manager job?

15. Who are the only two players to play for the Republic whose surname starts with the letter I?

16. Who did Ireland beat on penalties to reach the quarterfinal of the 1990 World Cup?

17. Ireland's biggest ever victory was an 8-0 thrashing of which country in 1983?

18. Who did Jack Charlton succeed as manager of the Irish team?

19. Which team wasn't in Ireland's Euro 2012 qualifying group?
    a) Russia
    b) Slovakia
    c) Slovenia

20. What is Ireland's highest ever position in the FIFA World Rankings?
    a) 6
    b) 8
    c) 10

EASY

Answers to Quiz 25: Pot Luck

1. Cameroon
2. Great Britain
3. Trevor Francis
4. Hull City
5. Lion
6. Dimitar Berbatov
7. Birmingham City
8. West Ham United
9. World Cup Willie
10. Heart of Midlothian
11. Roberto di Matteo
12. Ian Holloway
13. Real Sociedad
14. Libya's Colonel Gaddafi (his son is Al-Saadi Gaddafi)
15. The Hatters
16. Alan Ball
17. Twice
18. London and Manchester (Arsenal and Chelsea)
19. 3rd
20. Genoa

Quiz 27: Pot Luck

1. Which Cameroon international collapsed and died during a match against Colombia in 2003?

2. What is the most easterly club in England's top four divisions?

3. Matt Le Tissier is from which of the Channel Islands?

4. Which British teenager has been sold for the highest transfer fee?

5. Which goalkeeper famously performed the 'scorpion kick' at Wembley in 1995?

6. Bafana Bafana is the nickname of which international team?

7. Which club play their home games at Bramall Lane?

8. Which Liverpool legend said, 'Mind you, I've been here during the bad times too – one year we came second'?

9. How many top flight titles did Bobby Moore win?

10. Alan Smith started his career at Leeds. What other clubs has he played for?

11. Who were the unlikely winners of the 2012 Scottish League Cup?

12. Which team runs out to the theme tune from 1960s cop show Z Cars?

13. Which Dutch defender, who had a brief spell at Chelsea, is nicknamed The Cannibal?

14. Who said of his time as England manager, 'It was difficult in the beginning, in the middle and at the end'?

15. At what English ground will you find a statue of Ted Bates?

16. How did Argentina's Martin Palermo make the record books in a game against Colombia in 1999?

17. Who are the only British club to win the European Cup Winners' Cup more than once?

18. Who said, 'If God had wanted us to play football in the sky, He'd have put grass up there'?

19. How many English clubs have won the Fairs Cup / UEFA Cup?
    a) 5
    b) 6
    c) 7

20. What time was the kick-off of the 2012 FA Cup final?
    a) 3pm
    b) 5.15pm
    c) 7.45pm

Answers to Quiz 26: Republic of Ireland

1. 1988
2. Steve Staunton
3. Roy Keane
4. Iran
5. England
6. Italy
7. Robbie Keane
8. Johnny Giles
9. Kevin Sheedy
10. Kevin Kilbane
11. Spain
12. Argentina
13. Shay Given
14. Red Bull Salzburg
15. Steven Ireland and Denis Irwin
16. Romania
17. Malta
18. Eoin Hand
19. Slovenia
20. 6

Quiz 28: Grounds

Which clubs play at the following grounds?

1. Adams Park

2. Pride Park

3. The City Ground

4. Whaddon Road

5. Edgar Street

6. Edgeley Park

7. Bescot Stadium

8. Deepdale

9. The Kassam Stadium

10. Brisbane Road

11. Home Park

12. Dean Court

13. Griffin Park

14. Meadow Lane

15. Roots Hall

EASY

16. Moss Rose

17. Priestfield Stadium

18. Sincil Bank

19. Ashton Gate

20. Victoria Park

Answers to Quiz 27: Pot Luck

1. Marc-Vivien Foé
2. Norwich City
3. Guernsey
4. Wayne Rooney
5. Rene Higuita
6. South Africa
7. Sheffield United
8. Bob Paisley
9. None
10. Newcastle United, Manchester United and MK Dons
11. Kilmarnock
12. Everton
13. Khalid Boulahrouz
14. Steve McClaren
15. Southampton's St Mary's Stadium
16. He missed a hat trick of penalties
17. Chelsea in 1971 and 1998
18. Brian Clough
19. 6 – Leeds, Newcastle, Arsenal, Tottenham, Liverpool and Ipswich
20. 5.15pm

Quiz 29: Pot Luck

1. Who was Arsene Wenger describing when he said, 'He is like a PlayStation player. He is the best in the world by some distance'?

2. Roy of the Rovers played for which club?

3. Which team has won the League Cup the most times?

4. Who was the first English player to be sold for a fee of over £10m?

5. At which English ground will you find the Holte End?

6. Who did Martin Jol succeed as Fulham manager?

7. The Racecourse Ground is the home of which Welsh club?

8. Which international team holds the record for going the longest time without scoring a goal?

9. Roy Hodgson has managed which four Premier League clubs?

10. Which English defender was sold for a fee of £29.1m in 2002?

11. Liverpool signed Luis Suarez from which club?

12. Which club won a hat trick of Scottish Cups in 1982, 1983 and 1984?

13. Which West Ham legend was knighted in 2004?

14. How much did Real Madrid pay Manchester United to sign Cristiano Ronaldo?

15. Celtic won nine consecutive Scottish titles under the stewardship of which manager?

16. Which English defender scored an own goal and was then sent off on his Real Madrid debut?

17. Where did Celtic play their home games in 1994/95?

18. Which Tottenham midfielder had a 'goal' not given against Manchester United in 2004 despite the ball clearly crossing the line?

19. Which club has Tony Pulis not managed?
    a) Bournemouth
    b) Bristol City
    c) Bristol Rovers

20. Cristiano Ronaldo joined Manchester United from which club?
    a) Benfica
    b) Porto
    c) Sporting Lisbon

Answers to Quiz 28: Grounds

1.	Wycombe Wanderers	11.	Plymouth Argyle
2.	Derby County	12.	Bournemouth
3.	Nottingham Forest	13.	Brentford
4.	Cheltenham Town	14.	Notts County
5.	Hereford United	15.	Southend United
6.	Stockport County	16.	Macclesfield Town
7.	Walsall	17.	Gillingham
8.	Preston	18.	Lincoln City
9.	Oxford United	19.	Bristol City
10.	Leyton Orient	20.	Hartlepool United

EASY

Quiz 30: Nicknames part 2

Can you identify the following football figures from their nickname?

1. Big Eck

2. Ibracadabra

3. The Black Spider

4. Mighty Mouse

5. Sparky

6. Captain America

7. El Nino

8. Duncan Disorderly

9. Goldenballs

10. Jinky

11. Incredible Sulk

12. Sniffer

13. One Size

14. Romford Pele

15. The Non-Flying Dutchman

16. Psycho

17. Razor

18. The Atomic Flea

19. Bites Yer Legs

20. El pibe de oro (Golden Boy)

Answers to Quiz 29: Pot Luck

1. Lionel Messi
2. Melchester Rovers
3. Liverpool
4. Alan Shearer for £15m
5. Villa Park
6. Mark Hughes
7. Wrexham
8. Northern Ireland
9. Blackburn, Fulham, Liverpool and West Bromwich Albion
10. Rio Ferdinand
11. Ajax
12. Aberdeen
13. Sir Trevor Brooking
14. £80m
15. Jock Stein
16. Jonathan Woodgate
17. Hampden Park
18. Pedro Mendes
19. Bristol Rovers
20. Sporting Lisbon

Quiz 31: Pot Luck

1. With 27 domestic titles, Grasshopper is the most successful club in which European country?

2. Who famously said of the closing stages of the 2003 Premier League season, 'It's squeaky-bum time'?

3. Which Dane scored a hat trick of penalties in a League Cup tie against Coventry in 1986?

4. In 1984, which Ipswich striker became the youngest player to score in an English top-flight game?

5. Who did Neil Warnock succeed as manager of Leeds United in 2012?

6. How much did Liverpool pay Newcastle to secure the services of Andy Carroll?

7. Which team has won the most English top flight titles?

8. Who was fined by UEFA for revealing a t-shirt saying 'Dockers' after scoring a goal in a Cup Winners' Cup tie?

9. Which former Leicester City player captained Greece to Euro 2004 victory?

10. Who are the three non-Englishmen to have managed West Ham United?

11. True or false – Lionel Messi is named after soul singer Lionel Richie?

12. The Spice Boys was a nickname for the players of which club?

13. Which former Ipswich, Spurs and Manchester United striker hosts the breakfast show on radio station Talk Sport?

14. Willem II and AZ Alkmaar are clubs from which country?

15. What trophy is nicknamed La Orejona (big ears) in Spain?

16. Who did Craig Levein succeed as manager of the Scotland national team?

17. England defender Gary Cahill started his Premier League career with which club?

18. Alex Ferguson spent £4.5m on which Italian goalkeeper who played just four games for the club?

19. Which team has been in England's top division since 1919?
    a) Arsenal
    b) Everton
    c) Liverpool

20. How many British clubs won the European Cup Winners' Cup?
    a) 7
    b) 8
    c) 9

Answers to Quiz 30: Nicknames part 2

1. Alex McLeish
2. Zlatan Ibrahimovic
3. Lev Yashin
4. Kevin Keegan
5. Mark Hughes
6. Claudio Reyna
7. Fernando Torres
8. Duncan Ferguson
9. David Beckham
10. Jimmy Johnstone
11. Nicolas Anelka
12. Allan Clarke
13. Fitz Hall
14. Ray Parlour
15. Dennis Bergkamp
16. Stuart Pearce
17. Neil Ruddock
18. Lionel Messi
19. Norman Hunter
20. Diego Maradona

Quiz 32: Sponsors

Identify the Premier League club by their 2012 shirt sponsor:

1. Investec

2. Sportingbet

3. Air Asia

4. Tombola

5. Standard Chartered

6. 188Bet

7. Chang

8. Emirates

9. FX Pro

10. Samsung

11. Genting Casinos

12. AON

13. Aviva

14. Britannia

15. Etihad Airways

EASY

16. Bodog

17. 32Red

18. 12 Bet

19. Virgin Money

20. Prince's Trust

Answers to Quiz 31: Pot Luck

1. Switzerland
2. Alex Ferguson
3. Jan Molby
4. Jason Dozzell
5. Simon Grayson
6. £35m
7. Manchester United
8. Robbie Fowler
9. Theo Zagorakis
10. Lou Macari, Gianfranco Zola and Avram Grant

11. True
12. Liverpool
13. Alan Brazil
14. Holland
15. The European Cup
16. George Burley
17. Aston Villa
18. Massimo Taibi
19. Arsenal
20. 9

Quiz 33: Pot Luck

EASY

1. Which controversial striker said, 'Rooney's good but not the best in Manchester'?

2. Purely Belter was a 2000 film about two teenagers trying to get enough money to buy season tickets for which club?

3. Who is the youngest player to be sent off in a Premier League match?

4. When asked, 'What would you be if you weren't a footballer?', what was Peter Crouch's reply?

5. What is Somerset's only Football League club?

6. Frank Lampard enjoyed a loan spell at which club in 1995/96?

7. Which Sunderland striker made his England debut against Holland in 2012?

8. Liverpool beat which Championship club in the 2001 League Cup final?

9. The Clock End was a feature of which famous football ground?

10. McDiarmid Park is the home ground of which Scottish club?

11. Jose Mourinho was manager of which club before taking over at Real Madrid?

12. Robbie Fowler has played for which five British clubs?

13. Which rock star said of Manchester City's 6-1 win over United, 'I think the fact that Sir Alex Ferguson rested Howard Webb had a lot to do with the result'?

14. Which goalkeeper severed a tendon after dropping a bottle of salad cream on his foot?

15. Which three managers have been in charge at both Derby County and Nottingham Forest?

EASY

16. Which Northern Irish defender made his FA Cup debut in the 2004 final against Manchester United?

17. Who collected thousands of euros of parking fines after leaving his Porsche at a Spanish railway station, shortly before returning to the Premier League?

18. Which Ipswich goalkeeper saved eight of the ten penalties he faced in 1979/80?

19. For how long is a goalkeeper allowed to hold on to the ball?
    a) 4 seconds
    b) 6 seconds
    c) 8 seconds

20. Shakhtar Donetsk are based in which country?
    a) Poland
    b) Russia
    c) Ukraine

Answers to Quiz 32: Sponsors

1. Tottenham
2. Wolverhampton Wanderers
3. QPR
4. Sunderland
5. Liverpool
6. Bolton Wanderers
7. Everton
8. Arsenal
9. Fulham
10. Chelsea
11. Aston Villa
12. Manchester United
13. Norwich City
14. Stoke City
15. Manchester City
16. West Bromwich Albion
17. Swansea City
18. Wigan Athletic
19. Newcastle United
20. Blackburn Rovers

MEDIUM QUIZZES

Quiz 34: Pot Luck

1. What do the initials FIFA stand for?

2. Who was the first goalkeeper to save a penalty in a Wembley FA Cup final?

3. Norwich striker Grant Holt joined the Canaries from which club?

4. Lying 551 feet above sea level, which league club's ground is the highest in England?

5. Which Arsenal team mate said, 'For Tony Adams to admit he's an alcoholic took an awful lot of bottle'?

6. St George's Park National Football Centre is in which Midlands town?

7. In what decade did Liverpool win the FA Cup for the first time?

8. Prior to their 2011 FA Cup triumph, in what year did Manchester City last win a major trophy?

9. Which former Premier League referee was a teacher at Harrow School?

10. Barwuah is the middle name of which controversial striker?

11. Which ground hosted the best attended English top-flight game in history?

12. Which five stadiums have hosted a World Cup final and the Summer Olympics?

13. Who is the only Coventry City player to win the Premier League Golden Boot award?

14. Which country won the Olympic football gold medals at the 1912 games?

15. Darius Vassell, Kevin Campbell and Les Ferdinand all had spells playing in which foreign country?

16. Who was the manager of the Southampton side that defeated Manchester United 6-3 in 1996?

17. Which two British clubs beat Real Madrid in the European Cup Winners' Cup final?

18. Only one club has appeared in European competition every year since 1955. Can you name them?

19. What was the last club other than Celtic or Rangers to win the league in Scotland?
    a) Aberdeen
    b) Dundee United
    c) Hearts

20. In what decade was UEFA founded?
    a) 1930s
    b) 1940s
    c) 1950s

Answers to Quiz 67: League Cup

1. Rotherham
2. Chelsea's Gianluca Vialli
3. Middlesbrough
4. Norwich and Birmingham
5. Liverpool in 2001
6. Nottingham Forest 1978, Liverpool 1982, 1983 and 1984, Chelsea 2005 and Manchester United 2009
7. Sunderland
8. Tottenham's Juande Ramos
9. Nikola Zigic and Obafemi Martins
10. Wolves
11. Tottenham
12. Swindon Town and QPR
13. West Ham, Tottenham, Everton and Manchester United
14. Leicester City
15. Darren Ambrose
16. Clive Allen
17. QPR
18. Kolo Toure, Emmanuel Adebayor and John Obi Mikel
19. Chelsea
20. Brian Little

MEDIUM

Quiz 35: Premier League

1. Which Nigerian striker was named Premier League Player of the Month for April 2011 and February 2012?

2. Manchester United and Spurs have both scored nine goals in a game. Who were their opponents?

3. Aged 43 years and 5 months, who is the oldest player to play in the Premier League?

4. Who was the first player to score a Premier League hat trick?

5. Which club were runners-up in the first Premier League season?

6. Who was the first Asian player to receive a Premier League winner's medal?

7. Who ended Chelsea's 86-game unbeaten home run in October 2008?

8. Which Tottenham defender scored the fastest goal in Premier League history against Bradford in 2000?

9. Which team were relegated in 2001/02 after finishing fifth the previous season?

10. Who were the last team to field an all-English XI in a Premier League game?

11. Which defender was voted PFA Player of the Year in the first Premier League season?

12. In 2012, which team became the first in 11 years to beat Manchester United and Arsenal in consecutive games?

13. Who was the manager of Chelsea when the Premier League began in 1992?

14. Who got into trouble in 2011 for tweeting a picture of Howard Webb in a Manchester United kit?

15. Up to 2010/11, only five Englishmen had been named Premier League Player of the Season. Can you name them?

16. Who was the first non-English player to score 100 Premier League goals?

17. Who became the 21st member of the Premier League's 100-goal club in February 2012?

18. Who were the original sponsors of the Premier League?

19. Which team holds the record for the fewest points earned in a Premier League season?
    a) Bradford City
    b) Coventry City
    c) Derby County

20. Between May 2003 and October 2004, Arsenal went unbeaten in the Premier League for how many games?
    a) 47
    b) 48
    c) 49

MEDIUM

Answers to Quiz 34: Pot Luck

1. Fédération Internationale de Football Association or in English International Federation of Association Football
2. Dave Beasant
3. Shrewsbury Town
4. West Bromwich Albion's The Hawthorns
5. Ian Wright
6. Burton-on-Trent
7. 1960s
8. 1976
9. David Elleray
10. Mario Ballotelli
11. Maine Road
12. Olympiastadion Berlin, Wembley, Rome's Stadio Olimpico, Mexico City's Azteca Stadium and Munich's Olympiastadion
13. Dion Dublin (he shared the award in 1997/98)
14. Great Britain
15. Turkey
16. Graeme Souness
17. Chelsea and Aberdeen
18. Barcelona
19. Aberdeen
20. 1950s

Quiz 36: Pot Luck

1. Which English club is nicknamed The Glovers?

2. Who was the first England player to be sent off in the World Cup finals?

3. Goalkeeper David de Gea joined Manchester United from which club?

4. Which Everton defender was sent off in the 2010 World Cup final?

5. Who has played in all four English divisions, the Conference, the Champions League, the UEFA Cup and the World Cup?

6. Which five English clubs did Brian Clough manage?

7. Who scored the winning goal in the 2011 FA Cup final?

8. Brazilian defender David Luiz joined Chelsea from which club?

9. Who won the Football Writers' Player of the Year award in 2011 despite playing for a club that was relegated?

10. What was the venue for the worst attended game in the history of the Premier League?

11. Who was sacked as Liverpool's Director of Football in 2012?

12. Which Newcastle midfielder received a record-equalling 14 yellow cards in the 2010/11 season?

13. Which team won the second tier of English football in 1975?

14. Former Grimsby midfielder Curtis Woodhouse gave up professional football in 2006 to take up what sport?

15. Who were Manchester United's opponents in the game just prior to the Munich air crash?

16. Who is the youngest player to play for Arsenal in the Premier League?

17. Which goalkeeper made only his second first team appearance in Aston Villa's 1982 European Cup final triumph?

18. Which team won the 2011 Women's World Cup?

19. How many teams make up the German Bundesliga?
    a) 16
    b) 18
    c) 20

20. Which club were relegated in three successive seasons between 1979 and 1982?
    a) Bristol City
    b) Northampton Town
    c) Swansea City

MEDIUM

Answers to Quiz 35: Premier League

1. Peter Odemwingie
2. Ipswich and Wigan
3. John Burridge
4. Eric Cantona
5. Aston Villa
6. Park Ji-Sung
7. Liverpool
8. Ledley King
9. Ipswich Town
10. Aston Villa in 1999
11. Paul McGrath
12. Wigan
13. Ian Porterfield
14. Ryan Babel
15. Alan Shearer, Michael Owen, Kevin Phillips, Frank Lampard and Wayne Rooney
16. Dwight Yorke
17. Darren Bent
18. Carling
19. Derby County with 11 in 2007/08
20. 49

Quiz 37: Champions League/ European Cup

1. How many Italians were in Inter Milan's starting line-up in the 2010 final?

2. Who scored Aston Villa's winner in the 1982 European Cup final?

3. In 2003, the first all-Italian final took place. Which two teams were involved?

4. What is the only city to have provided two Champions Cup-winning teams?

5. Who was the first manager to win the European Cup three times?

6. Which Englishman scored a hat trick in just nine minutes against Rosenborg in 1995/96?

7. Who was Liverpool's goalkeeper in their 2005 penalty shoot-out victory over AC Milan?

8. Barcelona won their first European Cup at Wembley in 1992. Who did they beat in the final?

9. Porto beat which team in the 2004 final to give Jose Mourinho his first Champions League win?

10. Which manager led Liverpool to victory in the 1984 European Cup?

11. Which club did Nottingham Forest beat to win their first European Cup in 1979?

12. Who scored for Arsenal in their 2-1 final defeat at the hands of Barcelona in 2006?

13. Bayern Munich beat which team 7-0 in the last 16 of the 2011/12 Champions League?

14. Who was the first player to win the Champions League with three different clubs?

15. Which two Chelsea players missed penalties in their 2008 final loss to Manchester United?

16. In what year was the first European Cup final?

17. Who scored the winner in the 1981 European Cup final and the decisive penalty in the 1984 final shoot-out?

18. Who were the first team to win the competition despite not having won their domestic league the previous season nor being the defending champions?

19. Liverpool put eight past which Turkish club in the 2007/08 competition?
    a) Besiktas
    b) Galatasaray
    c) Fenerbaçhe

20. Which country has provided the highest number of different winning clubs?
    a) England
    b) Italy
    c) Spain

Answers to Quiz 36: Pot Luck

1. Yeovil Town
2. Ray Wilkins in 1986
3. Atletico Madrid
4. Johnny Heitinga
5. Steve Finnan
6. Hartlepool, Derby, Brighton, Leeds and Nottingham Forest
7. Yaya Touré
8. Benfica
9. Scott Parker
10. Selhurst Park
11. Damien Comolli
12. Cheik Tiote
13. Manchester United
14. Boxing
15. Red Star Belgrade
16. Jack Wilshere
17. Nigel Spink
18. Japan
19. 18
20. Bristol City

MEDIUM

Quiz 38: Pot Luck

1. Who won international caps in football and cricket for Scotland?

2. Which English club was originally known as Small Heath Alliance?

3. In what year was three points for a win introduced in English league games?

4. Who was the first Englishman to manage a top-flight club in Germany?

5. Jimmy Greaves played for which four clubs?

6. Who are the four Welshman to have won the PFA Player of the Year award?

7. Goalkeeper Joe Hart started his professional career with which club?

8. Swansea reached the Premier League for the first time after beating which club in the 2011 Play-Off final?

9. The Spireites is the nickname of which Football League club?

10. Sunderland paid which club £8m to gain the services of teenage striker Connor Wickham?

11. Which team put eight past Manchester City on the final day of the 2007/08 season?

12. Which manager led Aston Villa to the top-flight title in 1980/81?

13. Which silky midfielder scored a record-breaking 42 penalties for Liverpool between 1984 and 1995?

14. Superbia in Proelio is the motto of which Premier League club?

15. What is the third-largest club ground in England?

16. Paul Lambert took over as Norwich manager after a spell at which club?

17. Which team reached a European final in four successive years in the 1990s but won only once?

18. What happened in England's opening 1966 World Cup match against Uruguay that had never happened before?

19. With 138 matches in charge, who has managed England in the most games?
    a) Bobby Robson
    b) Alf Ramsey
    c) Walter Winterbottom

20. Who were the first team other than Real Madrid to win the European Cup?
    a) Benfica
    b) Inter Milan
    c) Sporting Lisbon

MEDIUM

Answers to Quiz 37: Champions League/European Cup

1.	None	11.	Malmö FF
2.	Peter Withe	12.	Sol Campbell
3.	AC Milan and Juventus	13.	Basel
4.	Milan	14.	Clarence Seedorf
5.	Bob Paisley	15.	Anelka and Terry
6.	Mike Newell	16.	1956
7.	Jerzy Dudek	17.	Alan Kennedy
8.	Sampdoria	18.	Manchester United in 1999
9.	Monaco	19.	Besiktas
10.	Joe Fagan	20.	England with six

Quiz 39: The FA Cup

1. Which Leicester City striker was the leading FA Cup goal-scorer in the 2011/12 season?

2. Which non-league team dumped top-flight Coventry City out of the Cup in 1989?

3. Who were the last team from outside the top flight to win the FA Cup?

4. Which third flight team reached the semifinals in 2001?

5. Who was the first man to miss a penalty in a Wembley FA Cup final?

6. Ricky Villa famously scored twice in the 1981 FA Cup final replay but who scored Tottenham's other goal?

7. In what year did the first all-Merseyside FA Cup final take place?

8. Who was the first Frenchman to lift the Cup as captain?

9. Which two clubs in the 20th century won the FA Cup in consecutive seasons?

10. Who is the only man to have captained FA Cup-winning teams in England and Scotland?

11. Which Premier League manager scored the winner in the 1990 Cup semifinal?

12. Who scored for Everton after just 25 seconds in the 2009 FA Cup Final?

13. In what year did Liverpool meet Newcastle in the final?

14. Who scored Manchester United's winning goal in the 1990 FA Cup final?

15. Which Everton and Sunderland midfielder played in four FA Cup finals and lost every one?

16. What connects Man City in 1926, Leicester in 1969, Brighton in 1983, Middlesbrough in 1997 and Portsmouth in 2010?

17. In 1983, who became the youngest player to score in an FA Cup final, aged just 18 years and 19 days?

18. What is the furthest round a non-league club has reached in the FA Cup?

19. Which of the following teams has not won the FA Cup?
    a) Birmingham City
    b) Bradford City
    c) Bury

20. Which ground has hosted the most FA Cup semifinals?
    a) Hillsborough
    b) Maine Road
    c) Villa Park

MEDIUM

Answers to Quiz 38: Pot Luck

1. Andy Goram
2. Birmingham City
3. 1981
4. Steve McClaren
5. Chelsea, AC Milan, Tottenham and West Ham
6. Ian Rush, Mark Hughes, Ryan Giggs and Gareth Bale
7. Shrewsbury Town
8. Reading
9. Chesterfield
10. Ipswich Town
11. Middlesbrough
12. Ron Saunders
13. Jan Molby
14. Manchester City
15. St James' Park, Newcastle
16. Colchester United
17. Juventus
18. England failed to score at Wembley
19. Walter Winterbottom
20. Benfica

Quiz 40: Pot Luck

1. Which two Spanish teams met in the final of the Europa League in 2012?

2. A dog in TV soap Coronation Street was named after which goalkeeper?

3. Striker Papiss Cissé joined Newcastle from which club?

4. The Biscuitmen was the former nickname of which English club?

5. Former England boss Graham Taylor started his managerial career at which club?

6. Which country won the gold medal in men's football at the 2004 and 2008 Olympics?

7. Which World Cup winner was the first player sold for a six-figure sum between English clubs?

8. Who was named Scottish PFA Player of the Year in 2011?

9. Which TV presenter stepped down from the commentary box to run the line in a match between Arsenal and Liverpool in 1972?

10. Which Premier League manager has a fascination with criminology and studied law at college before becoming a professional footballer?

11. Which player has taken part in the most losing World Cup penalty shoot-outs?

12. Who is France's most capped footballer?

13. Which superstitious Romanian striker always made sure his underwear was inside out while playing?

14. Just three countries have appeared in only one World Cup final. Can you name them?

15. Who were the first European Championships host country not to make it through the first round of the finals?

16. Which Croatian striker played in the 2008 European Championships despite having a kidney transplant in 2007?

17. Which Scottish club play their home games at Firhill Stadium?

18. Which eccentric manager has had spells in charge at Wimbledon, Iraq and Norway?

19. In the film Mike Bassett: England Manager, the eponymous hero was manager of which club before becoming the England boss?
    a) Ipswich Town
    b) Leicester City
    c) Norwich City

20. What is the minimum number of players each side must have on the pitch for a game to continue?
    a) 7
    b) 8
    c) 9

MEDIUM

Answers to Quiz 39: The FA Cup

1. Jermaine Beckford
2. Sutton United
3. West Ham in 1980
4. Wycombe Wanderers
5. John Aldridge
6. Garth Crooks
7. 1986
8. Eric Cantona
9. Newcastle and Tottenham
10. Martin Buchan
11. Alan Pardew
12. Louis Saha
13. 1974
14. Lee Martin
15. Paul Bracewell
16. They all lost in the final and got relegated in the same season
17. Norman Whiteside
18. Fifth
19. Birmingham City
20. Villa Park

Quiz 41: England

1. England's heaviest international defeat came at the hands of which country?

2. Which two managers took charge of England matches in the period between Kevin Keegan and Sven-Göran Eriksson?

3. Three players captained England in the 1990 World Cup finals. Name them.

4. True or false – England once wore a kit of yellow shirts, blue shorts and yellow socks?

5. This Time (We'll Get It Right) was the official team song from which World Cup?

6. Which manager led England to four World Cups?

7. Who was the first black player to captain England?

8. Which former England captain was born in Singapore?

9. England's first game under Roy Hodgson was a friendly against which country?

10. Who is the youngest player to score a hat trick for England?

11. Who were England's three opponents in the group stage of the 2010 World Cup?

12. Which England manager first appointed David Beckham captain of the national team?

13. Which 33-year-old made his England debut against Montenegro in October 2010?

14. Who succeeded Terry Venables as England manager?

15. England were eliminated from both Euro 2004 and World Cup 2006 by which team?

16. Two players with identical names were in England's 1986 World Cup squad. What was their name?

17. Who scored after just 27 seconds in England's World Cup game against France in 1982?

18. Who did England beat in a play-off to qualify for Euro 2000?

19. Which Newcastle striker scored five goals in an international against Cyprus?
    a) Les Ferdinand
    b) Malcolm Macdonald
    c) Alan Shearer

20. Who, in 2005, became the first player to be sent off twice for England?
    a) David Batty
    b) David Beckham
    c) Paul Ince

Answers to Quiz 40: Pot Luck

1. Atletico Madrid and Athletic Bilbao
2. Schmeichel
3. Freiburg
4. Reading
5. Lincoln City
6. Argentina
7. Alan Ball
8. Emilio Izaguirre
9. Jimmy Hill
10. Martin O'Neill
11. Roberto Baggio
12. Lilian Thuram
13. Adrian Mutu
14. England, Spain and Sweden
15. Belgium in 2000
16. Ivan Klasnic
17. Partick Thistle
18. Egil Olsen
19. Norwich City
20. 7

Quiz 42: Pot Luck

1.   Dennis Wise appeared in the FA Cup final for which three clubs?

2.   In what country was Roberto di Matteo born?

3.   Which country will host the 2016 European Championships?

4.   After managing England, Bobby Robson took over at which club?

5.   Which three England players scored in the 1990 penalty shoot-out defeat against West Germany?

6.   Which German team did Chelsea beat to win the 1998 European Cup Winners' Cup?

7.   Which team finished fourth in the 2010 World Cup?

8.   Who was the only Fulham player in the 1966 World Cup-winning team?

9.   Who made 365 consecutive league appearances for Liverpool between 1974 and 1983?

10. Which Scot failed a drug test at the 1978 World Cup?

11. What were players banned from wearing in 2011?

12. Crawley Town and what other team were promoted from the Conference in 2010/11?

13. In what year did England, Scotland, Northern Ireland and Wales all qualify for the World Cup finals?

14. Which club has won the Welsh Premier League the most times?

15. Which England international won eight league championship medals in England, France and Scotland?

16. What is the biggest margin of victory in an FA Cup match at Wembley?

17. What was the first British club to reach the semifinal of the European Cup?
    a) Dundee
    b) Hearts
    c) Hibernian

18. Which Newcastle striker scored 10 goals in his first six Premier League appearances?
    a) Papiss Cissé
    b) Mick Quinn
    c) Alan Shearer

Answers to Quiz 41: England

1. Hungary
2. Howard Wilkinson and Peter Taylor
3. Bryan Robson, Terry Butcher and Peter Shilton
4. True
5. Spain 1982
6. Walter Winterbottom
7. Paul Ince
8. Terry Butcher
9. Norway
10. Theo Walcott
11. USA, Algeria and Slovenia
12. Peter Taylor
13. Kevin Davies
14. Glenn Hoddle
15. Portugal
16. Gary Stevens
17. Bryan Robson
18. Scotland
19. Malcolm Macdonald
20. David Beckham

MEDIUM

Quiz 43: World Cup

1. England's 1990 semifinal against West Germany took place in which city?

2. Which country will host the 2018 World Cup?

3. In what year was the World Cup expanded from 24 to 32 teams?

4. Who won the World Cup hosted by Brazil in 1950?

5. Which Caribbean country qualified for the World Cup finals for the first time in 2006?

6. Who refereed the 2010 World Cup final?

7. In what year was the World Cup decided by a four-team mini group rather than a one-off final?

8. Which two London venues hosted matches in the 1966 World Cup?

9. Who is the oldest player to score in a World Cup finals match?

10. What was the name of the German-based octopus who correctly predicted a succession of results at the 2010 World Cup?

11. True or false – no team led by a foreign manager has won the World Cup?

12. What is the only stadium to have hosted two World Cup finals?

13. Just Fontaine scored 13 goals in the 1958 World Cup for which country?

14. Australia beat which country 31-0 in a qualifier for the 2002 World Cup?

15. In what year did England famously lose a World Cup match to America?

16. Who scored a hat trick in Italy's 3-2 win over the great Brazil side in the 1982 tournament?

17. Geoff Hurst scored England's first World Cup hat trick but who scored their second?

18. Which defender scored England's winner against Egypt in the group stage of the 1990 World Cup?

19. Which team humbled defending champions France in the opening match of the 2002 World Cup?
    a) Cameroon
    b) Ivory Coast
    c) Senegal

20. What was the most represented league at the 2010 World Cup?
    a) La Liga
    b) Premier League
    c) Serie A

MEDIUM

Answers to Quiz 42: Pot Luck

1. Wimbledon, Chelsea and Millwall
2. Switzerland
3. France
4. PSV Eindhoven
5. Gary Lineker, David Platt and Peter Beardsley
6. Stuttgart
7. Uruguay
8. George Cohen
9. Phil Neal
10. Willie Johnstone
11. Snoods
12. AFC Wimbledon
13. 1958
14. Barry Town
15. Trevor Steven
16. Stoke 5-0 Bolton in the 2011 semifinal
17. Hibernian
18. Mick Quinn

Quiz 44: Pot Luck

1. Which country hosted the 1954 World Cup?

2. Roberto di Matteo started his managerial career with which club?

3. In 1969, which two countries were involved in the so-called Football War?

4. True or false – Mario Balotelli is allergic to certain types of grass?

5. Who is the only Nottingham Forest player to have won the PFA Players' Player of the Year award?

6. Which English club won the first UEFA Cup?

7. Who was sent off in the 1998 World Cup final?

8. Which European team is unbeaten in four matches against Brazil, winning two and drawing two?

9. Which four teams in the top four divisions of English football have names that start and end with the same letter?

10. Aston Villa owner Randy Lerner also owns an NFL American football team. Which one?

11. Who scored goals in 10 consecutive Premier League games in 2003?

12. Which French World Cup-winner had a brief but successful spell at Birmingham City?

13. Which Newcastle defender scored in three successive games at the end of the 2010/11 season?

14. What name comes next – Brian Horton, Alan Ball, Steve Coppell?

15. Can you name two England internationals who have been capped since 1990 whose surname ends in the letter o?

16. What is Diego Maradona's middle name?

17. What is the nickname of the New Zealand national team?

18. In Italy, which two clubs share the Stadio Olimpico?

19. Dunga captained Brazil to World Cup glory but what does Dunga mean in Portuguese?
    a) Dopey
    b) Happy
    c) Sleepy

20. Who is France's all-time leading international goal scorer?
    a) Thierry Henry
    b) Michel Platini
    c) Just Fontaine

MEDIUM

Answers to Quiz 43: World Cup

1. Turin
2. Russia
3. 1998
4. Uruguay
5. Trinidad and Tobago
6. Howard Webb
7. 1950
8. Wembley and White City
9. Roger Milla
10. Paul
11. True
12. Azteca Stadium, Mexico City
13. France
14. American Samoa
15. 1950
16. Paolo Rossi
17. Gary Lineker
18. Mark Wright
19. Senegal
20. Premier League

Quiz 45: Bad Boys

1. In 1990, Pedro Monzon created which unwanted football record?

2. Which team received the most red cards in the 2010/11 Premier League season?

3. Which goalkeeper was sent off just 13 seconds into Sheffield Wednesday's game at Wolves in 2000?

4. Which former Premier League defender is the only man to be sent off in two World Cups?

5. In 2002, which Argentine striker became the first player to be sent off from the substitutes' bench during a World Cup match?

6. Which former Manchester United midfielder was jailed in 2011 for receiving stolen goods?

7. Paolo di Canio was given an 11-game ban for pushing over which referee?

8. Which striker served a 44-day prison term for headbutting an opponent in 1995?

9. Who was sent off in the 2011 FA Cup semifinal between Manchester City and Manchester United?

10. Which Middlesbrough defender was banned by UEFA for 18 months after failing a drug test?

11. Two Manchester United players have been given eight-month bans by the FA. Which two?

12. Which Newcastle team-mates were sent off for fighting each other in a game against Aston Villa in 2005?

13. Which former Everton, Manchester City and West Ham midfielder was jailed in 2005 for possession of cocaine with intent to supply?

14. Which two Frenchmen have been sent off in World Cup finals?

15. Who was sent off at each and every one of his five Premier League clubs?

16. Two Rangers players were banned from playing for Scotland for making offensive gestures at cameramen while on the bench for a game against Iceland. Name the pair.

17. Which Welsh midfielder was sentenced to 18 months in prison for his involvement in a counterfeit currency scam?

18. Three English Rangers players were sent off in a 1991 Scottish Cup against Celtic. Can you name them?

19. Which modern-day superstar was sent off two minutes into his international debut?
a) Lionel Messi
b) Cristiano Ronaldo
c) Wayne Rooney

20. How many cards did the referee show in the 2010 World Cup final?
a) 11
b) 13
c) 15

MEDIUM

Answers to Quiz 44: Pot Luck

1. Switzerland
2. MK Dons
3. Honduras and El Salvador
4. True
5. Peter Shilton
6. Tottenham Hotspur
7. Marcel Desailly
8. Norway
9. Liverpool, Charlton Athletic, Northampton Town, Aston Villa
10. Cleveland Browns
11. Ruud van Nistelrooy
12. Christophe Dugarry
13. Steven Taylor
14. Frank Clark (Manchester City managers)
15. Tony Dorigo and John Salako
16. Armando
17. The All Whites
18. AS Roma and Lazio
19. Dopey
20. Thierry Henry

Quiz 46: Pot Luck

1. Who was sent off for a deliberate handball in the closing stages of the 2010 World Cup quarterfinal between Ghana and Uruguay?

2. George Weah played for which two English clubs?

3. Who was the first player to win the Premier League with two different clubs?

4. Who won Britain's Brainiest Footballer in the 2002 TV show?

5. Schalke 04 are based in which German city?

6. Defender Kyle Walker joined Tottenham from which club?

7. Who did Aston Villa beat in the 1996 League Cup final?

8. Cristiano Ronaldo was born on which Atlantic island?

9. What nationality is Manchester United winger Antonio Valencia?

10. Which second-flight team beat Chelsea and Liverpool en route to the 2008 FA Cup semifinal?

11. Which club's crest features a globe sitting atop a football, draped in a ribbon?

12. Who holds the record for most appearances and goals by a Watford player?

13. Which manager of the French national team had a spell in charge at Tottenham?

14. Which six grounds hosted football matches at the 2012 London Olympics?

15. Which ball-playing defender was Gary Neville describing when he said, 'He plays football like he's being controlled by a 10-year-old on a PlayStation'?

16. The Honest Men is the nickname of which Scottish club?

17. Which recently-departed Brazilian legend was a qualified doctor?

18. Which Premier League player scored Australia's first ever World Cup finals goal?

19. Scottish tennis player Andy Murray is a fan of which club?
    a) Dundee United
    b) Hearts
    c) Hibernian

20. What lucky charm does goalkeeper Shay Given keep in his glove bag?
    a) four-leaf clover
    b) rabbit's foot
    c) a bottle of holy water

Answers to Quiz 45: Bad Boys

1. He was the first man to be sent off in a World Cup final
2. West Bromwich Albion
3. Kevin Pressman
4. Rigobert Song
5. Claudio Caniggia
6. Ronnie Wallwork
7. Paul Alcock
8. Duncan Ferguson
9. Paul Scholes
10. Abel Xavier
11. Eric Cantona and Rio Ferdinand
12. Lee Bowyer and Kieron Dyer
13. Mark Ward
14. Marcel Desailly and Zinedine Zidane
15. Carlton Palmer
16. Barry Ferguson and Allan McGregor
17. Mickey Thomas
18. Terry Hurlock, Mark Walters and Mark Hateley
19. Lionel Messi
20. 13

MEDIUM

Quiz 47: European Championship

1. What country won the first ever European Championships?

2. England won their first penalty shoot-out in Euro 96 against which team?

3. Which two countries were the first to co-host the European Championship finals?

4. Germany famously beat England in the semifinal of Euro 96 but who did they beat in the final?

5. Which former Liverpool and Aston Villa striker was the leading scorer at Euro 2004?

6. What is the only Scandinavian country to host the European Championships?

7. Which Frenchman scored nine goals in the 1984 tournament?

8. In what year did Scotland make their first European Championship finals appearance?

9. England have reached the semifinals twice. In 1996 and in what other year?

10. Who did Holland beat in the final of Euro 88?

11. Who did hosts England play in the opening match of Euro 96?

12. Who was the coach of the Spanish side that won in 2008?

13. Who scored for Ireland in their famous win over England at Euro 88?

14. What is the name of the trophy won by the winning team?

15. What were the eight grounds that hosted games at Euro 96?

16. The first England player to be sent off in an international saw red in the 1968 tournament. What was his name?

17. Which Arsenal midfielder scored the opening goal of the 1992 final?

18. Who scored the Golden Goal that gave France victory over Italy at Euro 2000?

19. Which country hosted the first European Championships?
    a) France
    b) Italy
    c) Spain

20. Up to 1980, how many teams took part in the European Championship finals?
    a) 4
    b) 8
    c) 16

MEDIUM

Answers to Quiz 46: Pot Luck

1. Luis Suarez
2. Chelsea and Manchester City
3. Henning Berg
4. Clark Carlisle
5. Gelsenkirchen
6. Sheffield United
7. Leeds United
8. Madeira
9. Ecuadorian
10. Barnsley
11. Birmingham City
12. Luther Blissett
13. Jacques Santini
14. City of Coventry Stadium (Ricoh Arena), Hampden Park, Wembley, Millennium Stadium, Old Trafford, St James' Park
15. David Luiz
16. Ayr United
17. Socrates
18. Tim Cahill
19. Hibernian
20. A bottle of holy water

Quiz 48: Pot Luck

1. Which international team fell foul of FIFA regulations by wearing sleeveless shirts?

2. Prepared is the motto of which Premier League club?

3. Who earned top-flight winners' medals with Everton in 1987 and Blackburn in 1995?

4. Who, in April 2012, was appointed manager of Chinese club Shanghai Shenhua?

5. Which Bolton striker won his one and only cap against Holland in 2002?

6. Who was the first Chelsea manager to work under Roman Abramovich?

7. Norwich's Simeon Jackson plays international football for which country?

8. Who were the first British side to win a European trophy?

9. Which three players from the Republic of Ireland have won the PFA Players' Player of the Year Award?

10. Which team did Tottenham beat in the 1984 UEFA Cup final?

11. Which goalscorer-turned-pundit launched a percussion instrument called the Dube?

12. Which prolific poacher is partial to completing 1,000-piece, equine-inspired jigsaws?

13. Wigan goalkeeper Ali Al-Habsi plays his international football for which country?

14. Who did Hull City beat in the 2007/08 Championship Play Off final?

15. Brian Clough led Derby to the first of two top-flight titles in the 1970s, but which manager led them to their second?

16. Which much-travelled British coach was appointed manager of FYR Macedonia in 2011?

17. Which Spanish side beat Leeds United in the Champions League semifinal 2001?

18. Which Lancashire club won the Conference in 2012?

19. Who is Southampton's all-time leading league goalscorer?
a) Mick Channon
b) Rickie Lambert
c) Matthew Le Tissier

20. Who scored the winning goal in Nottingham Forest's 1980 European Cup triumph over Hamburg?
a) Garry Birtles
b) Trevor Francis
c) John Robertson

MEDIUM

Answers to Quiz 47: European Championship

1. Soviet Union
2. Spain
3. Holland and Belgium in 2000
4. Czech Republic
5. Milan Baroš
6. Sweden (in 1992)
7. Michel Platini
8. 1992
9. 1968
10. USSR
11. Switzerland
12. Luis Aragonés
13. Ray Houghton
14. The Henri Delaunay Cup
15. Wembley, Villa Park, Old Trafford, City Ground, St James' Park, Anfield, Hillsborough, Elland Road
16. Alan Mullery
17. John Jensen
18. David Trezeguet
19. France
20. 4

Quiz 49: Managers

1. Which manager is credited with creating the Total Football style of play?

2. Norwich City secured their best ever Premier League finish in 1992/93 under which manager?

3. George Graham began his managerial career with which club?

4. Who was the last English manager before Harry Redknapp in 2008 to lead his team to FA Cup victory?

5. Who was the first manager from outside the British Isles to win a major English trophy?

6. Which Scot started his managerial career at St Johnstone then had spells at Dundee Utd, Plymouth, Southampton, Sheffield Wednesday, Swindon and Southend?

7. Who took over as manager of MK Dons in May 2010, aged just 29?

8. Who did Jose Mourinho replace as manager of Real Madrid?

9. David O'Leary managed Leeds United and what other Premier League club?

10. Which manager led the Dutch team to the 2010 World Cup final?

11. Which former physio started his English managerial career at Scunthorpe in 2006?

12. In which country will you find the Guus Hiddink Stadium?

13. Which England manager said, 'I was just saying to your colleague, the referee has got me the sack, thank him ever so much for that, won't you'?

14. Which British manager has had spells at Real Madrid, Real Sociedad, Besiktas, St Etienne, Catania and Real Murcia?

15. Which German international was appointed manager of Brentford in June 2011?

16. Who was the last English manager to win the European Cup?

17. Terry Venables and Bobby Robson are two of the three Englishmen to have managed Barcelona since the war. Who is the third?

18. Which manager steered France to World Cup glory in 1998?

19. How many days was Brian Clough in charge at Leeds United?
    a) 40
    b) 44
    c) 48

20. Who was the manager of the 1948 Great Britain Olympic football team?
    a) Matt Busby
    b) Bill Shankly
    c) Alf Ramsey

Answers to Quiz 48: Pot Luck

1. Cameroon
2. Aston Villa
3. Bobby Mimms
4. Nicolas Anelka
5. Michael Ricketts
6. Claudio Ranieri
7. Canada
8. Tottenham in the 1963 Cup Winners' Cup
9. Liam Brady, Paul McGrath and Roy Keane
10. Anderlecht
11. Dion Dublin
12. Michael Owen
13. Oman
14. Bristol City
15. Dave Mackay
16. John Toshack
17. Valencia
18. Fleetwood Town
19. Mick Channon
20. John Robertson

MEDIUM

Quiz 50: Pot Luck

1. True or false – a goal can be scored straight from the kick-off?

2. The Keepmoat Stadium is the home ground of which Football League club?

3. Ferenc Puskas played for which two countries at the finals of the World Cup?

4. Who is the only player to win top-flight English titles in consecutive seasons with different clubs?

5. Every game of the 1930 World Cup was played in which South American city?

6. Who was manager of Manchester City for just 33 days in 1996?

7. Plainmoor is the home ground of which English club?

8. Who scored a wonder goal for Norwich in their famous win over Bayern Munich in 1993?

9. What animal features on the Sunderland crest?

10. Which dapper coach took charge of the German national team in 2006?

11. Which player won eight consecutive league titles with five different clubs starting in 2003/04?

12. Who, after scoring in Manchester City's 6-1 win over city rivals United lifted his shirt to reveal the message 'Why Always Me?'

13. Who are the two uncapped Englishmen to play in a Champions League final?

14. Up to 2011, how many Italian players had won the Premier League?

Answers - page 105

15. Which Premier League club had a shirt sponsorship agreement with the Acorns Children's Hospice?

16. Fill in the blank: Sharp, Vodafone, _____, AON?

17. Former Manchester United, Leeds and Bradford winger Lee Sharpe had a brief spell at which Italian club?

18. There are MLS teams in which three Canadian cities?

19. Which country has won the Africa Cup of Nations the most times?
    a) Cameroon
    b) Egypt
    c) Ghana

20. Which of the following countries has never qualified for the World Cup finals?
    a) Canada
    b) Finland
    c) Israel

MEDIUM

Answers to Quiz 49: Managers

1. Rinus Michels
2. Mike Walker
3. Millwall
4. Joe Royle in 1995
5. Ruud Gullit
6. Paul Sturrock
7. Karl Robinson
8. Manuel Pellegrini
9. Aston Villa
10. Bert van Marwijk
11. Nigel Adkins
12. South Korea
13. Graham Taylor
14. John Toshack
15. Uwe Rosler
16. Joe Fagan
17. Vic Buckingham
18. Aimé Jacquet
19. 44
20. Matt Busby

Quiz 51: Goalscorers

1. Which prolific English striker was once exchanged for a set of weights?

2. Rickie Lambert joined Southampton from which club?

3. Who is the only post-war player to score 30 top-flight goals in three successive seasons?

4. The Vulture was the nickname of which prolific Spanish striker?

5. Who was the top scorer at the 2006 World Cup?

6. Who scored a hat trick in just 4m 30s against Arsenal in August 1994?

7. Edin Džeko plays international football for which country?

8. Who scored 23 goals in his first ten league games for Rangers in 1997?

9. Who, in 2006, became the first player to score at least 20 Premier League goals in five consecutive seasons?

10. Who scored seven goals for Oldham in a 1989 League Cup game against Scarborough?

11. Which Norwich striker was the first Englishman to score a hat trick in the Premier League?

12. Which much-travelled Kosovo-born striker started his career in England with Stockport County in 2001?

13. How many goals did Gary Lineker score in his England career?

14. John Atyeo scored 315 goals in the 1950s and 60s for which club?

15. Up to the start of the 2011/12 season, which four players had scored five goals in a single Premier League game?

16. Chris Sutton scored Premier League goals for which five clubs?

17. Who scored after just 10.8s in the 2002 World Cup 3rd/4th Place Play Off?

18. Fulham and England striker Andrew Johnson started his career with which club?

19. Andrily Shevchenko joined Chelsea from which club?
    a) AC Milan
    b) Dynamo Kiev
    c) Juventus

20. Who is England's leading goal-scorer in competitive internationals?
    a) Bobby Charlton
    b) Gary Lineker
    c) Michael Owen

MEDIUM

Answers to Quiz 50: Pot Luck

1. True
2. Doncaster Rovers
3. Hungary and Spain
4. Eric Cantona
5. Montevideo
6. Steve Coppell
7. Torquay United
8. Jeremy Goss
9. Lion
10. Joachim Löw
11. Zlatan Ibrahimovic
12. Mario Balotelli
13. Jermaine Pennant and Ryan Bertrand
14. None
15. Aston Villa
16. AIG (Manchester United shirt sponsors)
17. Sampdoria
18. Toronto, Vancouver and Montreal
19. Egypt
20. Finland

Quiz 52: Pot Luck

1. How much additional time does a referee allow for each substitution made during a half?

2. What was the first team to complete the league and FA Cup double?

3. Peter Crouch made his English league debut with which club?

4. What was Fabio Capello's last managerial job before becoming England manager?

5. Which two English clubs met in the 1972 UEFA Cup final?

6. The Saddlers is the nickname of which English club?

7. Which Aston Villa keeper let a throw-in roll under his foot to gift Birmingham a goal in 2002?

8. Newcastle United's crest features a lion and what other animal?

9. Which team has received the most red cards in World Cup history?

10. Which international manager said the following after the first leg of the Euro 2012 play-offs, 'Be careful of the cat. Don't say you have the cat in the sack when you don't have the cat in the sack'?

11. Who scored the only goal in England's 1-0 win over Spain in 2012?

12. Who are the only two Welshman to have played top-flight football in Italy?

13. Before becoming a full-time referee what was Howard Webb's occupation?

14. Which goalkeeper was the last player to move directly from Manchester City to Manchester United?

15. Who scored six goals in an FA Cup match and still ended up on the losing side?

16. Which team won the MLS Cup in 2011?

17. What is the Stadio Giuseppe Meazza more commonly known as?

18. Who were the first country to hold the World Cup and European Championships simultaneously?

19. In addition to Sheffield Wednesday, Dave Jones and Gary Megson have both managed which club?
    a) Cardiff City
    b) Stockport County
    c) Wolverhampton Wanderers

20. Which club wasn't involved in the first Premier League season?
    a) Crystal Palace
    b) Oldham Athletic
    c) Stoke City

MEDIUM

Answers to Quiz 51: Goalscorers

1. Ian Wright
2. Bristol Rovers
3. Alan Shearer
4. Emilio Butragueno
5. Miroslav Klose
6. Robbie Fowler
7. Bosnia and Herzegovina
8. Marco Negri
9. Thierry Henry
10. Frankie Bunn
11. Mark Robins
12. Shefki Kuqi

13. 48
14. Bristol City
15. Alan Shearer, Andy Cole, Jermain Defoe and Dimitar Berbatov
16. Norwich, Blackburn, Chelsea, Birmingham and Aston Villa
17. Hakan Sukur
18. Birmingham City
19. AC Milan
20. Michael Owen

Quiz 53: Grounds and Stadiums

1. The grounds of which two British clubs are closest together?

2. The Allianz Arena is home to which two German clubs?

3. What was the first ground in England with undersoil heating?

4. Where did Manchester United play the home leg of their European Cup Winners' Cup tie against St Etienne in October 1977?

5. What was the first all-seater ground in Britain?

6. The highest ever attendance for a World Cup game was 199,850. Who were playing and where?

7. The Gwladys Street Stand is at which ground?

8. Which Scottish Club play at East End Park?

9. At which ground will you find the Tilton Road End?

10. Brighton shared which club's ground from 1997 to 1999?

11. At what ground did 'Coracle Man' recover balls kicked over the stands?

12. Which London ground is located on Holmesdale Road?

13. Which Spanish club calls the Vicente Calderón Stadium home?

14. The highest attendance at a domestic game in Britain occurred at which ground?

15. Windsor Park is the home ground of which Northern Irish club?

16. What is the only club to play in an FA Cup final at five different grounds?

17. Which European club plays their home games at Estadio da Luz?

18. What is the most southerly league ground in England?

19. Which ground was once known as 'The Wembley of the North'?
    a) City Ground
    b) Deepdale
    c) Vale Park

20. Stanley Matthews' ashes are buried under the centre circle at which ground?
    a) Bloomfield Road
    b) Britannia Stadium
    c) Wembley

Answers to Quiz 52: Pot Luck

1. 30 seconds
2. Preston North End
3. QPR
4. Real Madrid
5. Tottenham Hotspur and Wolverhampton Wanderers
6. Walsall
7. Peter Enckelman
8. Seahorse
9. Brazil
10. Giovanni Trapattoni
11. Frank Lampard
12. John Charles and Ian Rush
13. Policeman
14. Tony Coton
15. Denis Law (the original match was abandoned and his Manchester City side lost the rearranged fixture)
16. LA Galaxy
17. The San Siro Stadium
18. West Germany
19. Stockport County
20. Stoke City

MEDIUM

Quiz 54: Pot Luck

1. Which Italian striker was Alex Ferguson describing when he said he 'was born in an offside position'?

2. True or false – Scotland's joint leading scorer, Denis Law, never played for a Scottish club?

3. Which English club were the last winners of the Inter City Fairs Cup?

4. Who was the last Englishman to win the Premier League Golden Boot award?

5. Which club were the first winners of the Football League in 1888?

6. BBC pundit Mark Lawrenson had a brief spell as manager of which club?

7. Who won the 2012 Johnstone's Paint Trophy?

8. George Best played league football in Scotland for which club?

9. The Alan Hardaker Trophy is awarded to the man of the match in which game?

10. Liverpool put ten past which Irish club in the 1969/70 Fairs Cup?

11. Clubs from the same country won the European Cup, Cup Winners' Cup and UEFA Cup in the same year only once. What country and which clubs?

12. Which publication is known as The Half Decent Football Magazine?

13. Uruguay's Jose Batista was sent off just 56 seconds into a 1986 World Cup game against which team?

14. Fabio Capello's last game in charge of England was a 1-0 win over which country?

15. Who has played in derby matches in South Wales, Merseyside, Manchester, East Anglia, the North East, London and Lancashire, not to mention the Old Firm?

16. Which Northern Ireland goalkeeper was born in Hildesheim, Germany?

17. Newcastle signed Fabricio Coloccini from which club?

18. Who is Holland's most capped player?

19. Who scored the winning goal in the Chelsea's 1-0 Champions League semifinal win over Barcelona at Stamford Bridge in 2012?
a) Didier Drogba
b) Frank Lampard
c) John Terry

20. In what year did Wales beat England at Wembley for the first time?
a) 1957
b) 1967
c) 1977

Answers to Quiz 53: Grounds and Stadiums

1. Dundee and Dundee United
2. Bayern Munich and 1860 Munich
3. Everton's Goodison Park
4. Plymouth's Home Park
5. Pittodrie
6. Brazil and Uruguay at the Maracana, Rio in the 1950 World Cup
7. Goodison Park
8. Dunfermline Athletic
9. Birmingham City
10. Gillingham
11. Shrewsbury's Gay Meadow
12. Crystal Palace's Selhurst Park
13. Atletico Madrid
14. Hampden Park
15. Linfield
16. Wolverhampton Wanderers
17. Benfica
18. Plymouth's Home Park
19. Vale Park
20. Britannia Stadium

MEDIUM

Quiz 55: Brits Abroad

1. Which Scot was manager of MLS side New England Revolution from 2002 until 2011?

2. Peter Reid was formerly the manager of which Asian country?

3. Joe Cole left Liverpool in 2011 to join which French club on loan?

4. Trevor Francis played for which two Italian clubs?

5. Which former Rangers, Everton and Chelsea striker is coach of the Portland Timbers MLS team?

6. Which European Cup winner managed Thailand from 1998 to 2002 and Indonesia from 2004 to 2007?

7. Prior to taking the England job, Roy Hodgson had managed which three countries?

8. Jermaine Pennant had a brief spell at which Spanish club?

9. Which Welsh striker-turned-manager had spells at Benfica and Galatasaray?

10. Who played abroad at Sampdoria and also had spells as manager of Torino, Galatasaray and Benfica?

11. Steve McClaren won the Dutch Eredivisie with which club?

12. Which former Tottenham defender has managed Pakistan and most recently Nepal?

13. Which diminutive winger had a spell in Italy at Reggiana?

14. Who was the first British player to win the Champions League / European Cup with a non-British team?

15. Which Scottish striker-turned-pundit played for Borussia Dortmund, Utrecht, Vitesse and FC Twente?

16. Which former Tottenham midfielder had spells in Canada, Hungary, Moldova, Germany and Republic of Ireland before returning to England in 2012?

17. Who are the five English players to have donned the famous white Real Madrid shirt?

18. Bobby Robson managed which four overseas clubs?

19. Ray Wilkins joined Rangers in 1987 from which club?
    a) AC Milan
    b) Marseille
    c) Paris St Germain

20. Which former England manager took over as boss of Bahrain in 2011?
    a) Glenn Hoddle
    b) Kevin Keegan
    c) Peter Taylor

Answers to Quiz 54: Pot Luck

1. Filippo Inzaghi
2. True
3. Leeds United
4. Kevin Phillips
5. Preston North End
6. Oxford United
7. Chesterfield
8. Hibernian
9. League Cup final
10. Dundalk
11. Italy in 1990 – AC Milan, Sampdoria and Juventus
12. When Saturday Comes
13. Scotland
14. Sweden
15. Craig Bellamy
16. Maik Taylor
17. Deportivo La Coruna
18. Edwin van der Sar
19. Didier Drogba
20. 1977

Quiz 56: Pot Luck

1. David Beckham has played for which five clubs?

2. Bill Shankly left which club to become the manager of Liverpool?

3. Bolton striker Kevin Davies started his career with which club?

4. Which four English clubs installed artificial pitches in the 1980s?

5. Players from which two teams were involved in an on-pitch brawl after a 2006 World Cup quarterfinal penalty shoot-out?

6. What was the best-attended World Cup tournament in history?

7. Which two Germans have scored 14 World Cup goals?

8. Which three Football League clubs that took part in the 2011/12 season had an X in their name?

9. What is the most northerly city to host a World Cup qualifier?

10. Which disciplinarian Argentina manager refused to pick players unless they had short hair?

11. Which Danish defender scored the first goal in Alex Ferguson's reign as Manchester United manager?

12. Which German, who scored in two World Cup finals, was nicknamed Der Afro?

13. Who is the only Dutch boss to win the Premier League Manager of the Month award?

14. Which manager said, 'We threw everything at them – the kitchen sink, golf clubs, emptied the garage. It wasn't enough but at least my garage is tidy now'?

15. How did Placido Galindo make history in Peru's 1930 World Cup game against Romania?

16. Can you name the eleven league clubs managed by Neil Warnock?

17. Which former Northern Ireland manager was the first man to be sent off for a professional foul?

18. On which country's badge will you find the letter KNVB?

19. Chic Brodie's career came to a premature end after he got injured by what?
a) a deckchair
b) a dog
c) an iron

20. Penarol, Nacional and Liverpool are clubs in which South American country?
a) Argentina
b) Chile
c) Uruguay

Answers to Quiz 55: Brits Abroad

1. Steve Nicol
2. Thailand
3. Lille
4. Sampdoria and Atalanta
5. John Spencer
6. Peter Withe
7. Switzerland, United Arab Emirates and Finland
8. Real Zaragoza
9. Dean Saunders
10. Graeme Souness
11. FC Twente
12. Graham Roberts
13. Franz Carr
14. Paul Lambert
15. Scott Booth
16. Rohan Ricketts
17. David Beckham, Steve McManaman, Michael Owen, Jonathan Woodgate and Laurie Cunningham
18. PSV Eindhoven (twice), Porto, Sporting Lisbon and Barcelona
19. Paris St Germain
20. Peter Taylor

MEDIUM

Quiz 57: Former Grounds

Can you identify which clubs used to call the following grounds home?

1. Fellows Park

2. Burnden Park

3. Vetch Field

4. Springfield Park

5. Boothferry Park

6. Eastville

7. Layer Road

8. Belle Vue

9. Leeds Road

10. Manor Ground

11. Elm Park

12. Millmoor

13. Old Showground

14. Gay Meadow

15. Victoria Ground

16. Highfield Road

17. The Dell

18. Ayresome Park

19. Roker Park

20. Goldstone Ground

Answers to Quiz 56: Pot Luck

1. Manchester United, Preston North End (loan), Real Madrid, LA Galaxy and AC Milan
2. Huddersfield Town
3. Chesterfield
4. Luton, Oldham, QPR and Preston
5. Argentina and Germany
6. USA 94
7. Gerd Muller and Miroslav Klose
8. Oxford United, Crewe Alexandra and Exeter City
9. Reykjavik
10. Daniel Passarella
11. John Sivebaek
12. Paul Breitner
13. Martin Jol
14. Ian Holloway
15. He was the first player sent off in the World Cup
16. Scarborough, Notts County, Torquay, Huddersfield, Plymouth, Oldham, Bury, Sheffield United, Crystal Palace, QPR and Leeds
17. Lawrie Sanchez
18. Holland
19. A dog
20. Uruguay

Quiz 58: Pot Luck

MEDIUM

1. Who captained Hull City in all four divisions?

2. Who scored a hat trick in just 140 seconds for Bournemouth against Wrexham in 2004?

3. Which Manchester United defender won two All-Ireland Gaelic Football titles with Dublin in 1975 and 1976?

4. Who is the only Scot to have been named European Footballer of the Year?

5. True or false – Japan have appeared in the Copa America?

6. Which team beat Arsenal in the 2000 UEFA Cup final?

7. Which Scottish club are nicknamed Blue Brazil?

8. Which striker, whose first name is also the capital city of a British Overseas Territory, scored 33 Premier League goals between 1997 and 2001?

9. Who, in 2007, became the first woman to commentate on a game for Match of the Day?

10. What tournament provided the backdrop for the classic film The Italian Job?

11. What appeared on shirts for the first time at the 1992 European Championships?

12. Brothers Johnny, Wilson and Jerry Palacios were all members of which country's squad at the 2010 World Cup?

13. In 2012, David Healy became Northern Ireland's most capped outfield player. Which defender's record did he beat?

14. Which team has lost the most Premier League games since the league's creation?

15. Sunderland's Stéphane Sessègnon plays international football for which country?

16. Who is the only Pakistan international to have played in the Premier League?

17. Which team reached the top 40 in 1978 with a version of We've Got The Whole World In Our Hands?

18. Which goalkeeper played for Liverpool between 1999 and 2001 and then had a brief spell at Everton in 2006?

19. Manchester United forward Javier Hernandez is nicknamed Chicharito but what does Chicharito mean?
    a) little dog
    b) little pea
    c) little worm

20. Which of the following big clubs has not won the Football League Trophy?
    a) Bolton
    b) Stoke
    c) Sheffield Wednesday

MEDIUM

Answers to Quiz 57: Former Grounds

1. Walsall
2. Bolton Wanderers
3. Swansea City
4. Wigan Athletic
5. Hull City
6. Bristol Rovers
7. Colchester United
8. Doncaster Rovers
9. Huddersfield Town
10. Oxford United
11. Reading
12. Rotherham United
13. Scunthorpe United
14. Shrewsbury Town
15. Stoke City
16. Coventry City
17. Southampton
18. Middlesbrough
19. Sunderland
20. Brighton and Hove Albion

Quiz 59: Scotland

1. Who are the Scotland team's joint top scorers?

2. How many times have Scotland qualified for the European Championships?

3. Kenny Dalglish is Scotland's most capped player. How many appearances did he make?

4. Who scored in Scotland's 1-0 win over England at Wembley in 1999?

5. Which Scotland manager was in charge for the most matches?

6. Scotland's biggest international win was an 11-0 thrashing of which country?

7. Who scored Scotland's only goal in their 4-1 defeat against Brazil in the 1982 World Cup?

8. Excluding Hampden, which ground has hosted the most Scottish home internationals?

9. How many World Cups have Scotland played at?

10. Who briefly took charge of the team after the resignation of Berti Vogts?

11. The first ever Scottish national team was made up entirely of players from which club?

12. Which manager led Scotland to the 1990 World Cup?

13. Archie Gemmill scored twice in Scotland's famous 3-2 win over Holland in 1978. Who scored the other goal?

14. Can you name a Scottish international whose surname ends in the letter A?

15. Who succeeded Jock Stein as manager of the national team?

16. Which team refused to play Scotland in a 1998 World Cup qualifier over a row about floodlights?

17. Who, in 1969, was the last person to score a hat trick for Scotland?

18. Scotland won one game at the 1990 World Cup. Who were their opponents?

19. In what year did the Tartan Army destroy the goalposts after a famous win at Wembley?
    a) 1975
    b) 1977
    c) 1979

20. Don't Come Home Too Soon was the official Scottish team song for which World Cup?
    a) 1982
    b) 1990
    c) 1998

MEDIUM

Answers to Quiz 58: Pot Luck

1. Ian Ashbee
2. James Hayter
3. Kevin Moran
4. Denis Law
5. True
6. Galatasaray
7. Cowdenbeath
8. Hamilton Ricard
9. Jacqui Oatley
10. The 1968 European Championships
11. Names of players
12. Honduras
13. Mal Donaghy
14. Everton
15. Benin
16. Zesh Rehman
17. Nottingham Forest
18. Sander Westerveld
19. Little pea
20. Sheffield Wednesday

Quiz 60: Pot Luck

1. What nationality is Reading goalkeeper Adam Federici?

2. Before taking over at Everton, David Moyes was the manager of which club?

3. Who were the first World Cup holders to also win the European Championship two years later?

4. In terms of capacity, what is the second-largest club ground in Britain?

5. Who are the only team to have played in the Premier League, the Championship, all four old divisions, Division 3 North and Division 3 South?

6. Which Northern Irish team were the first to be eliminated from European competition on away goals?

7. The PFA Fair Play award is named after which player?

8. What's the only English league team that doesn't have any of the letters from the word goal in its name?

9. Which two Scottish League clubs begin with the letter F?

10. Which former Birmingham City, Wigan Athletic and Blackpool player is Ghana's most capped player?

11. Who are the four Welshmen to have scored Premier League hat tricks?

12. Which legendary manager said, 'Of course I didn't take my wife to see Rochdale as an anniversary present. It was her birthday. Would I have got married in the football season? Anyway, it was Rochdale reserves'?

13. Which full back made 243 appearances for Liverpool without scoring?

14. Which goalkeeper was forced to withdraw from England's Euro 2012 squad after breaking a finger shortly before the tournament?

15. Which team defeated QPR to win the 1986 League Cup?

16. Which two teams featured in the first-ever episode of Match of the Day?

17. Scottish writer Irvine Welsh is a fan of which club?

18. Which Dutch legend was nicknamed The Swan of Utrecht?

19. What was used at a football ground for the first time in the 1920s?
    a) dugouts
    b) corner flags
    c) floodlights

20. Which of the following clubs wasn't a founder member of the Football League?
    a) Birmingham City
    b) West Bromwich Albion
    c) Wolverhampton Wanderers

Answers to Quiz 59: Scotland

1. Denis Law and Kenny Dalglish
2. Twice
3. 102
4. Don Hutchinson
5. Craig Brown with 71 games
6. Ireland
7. David Narey
8. Celtic Park
9. eight
10. Tommy Burns
11. Queen's Park
12. Andy Roxburgh
13. Kenny Dalglish
14. Christophe Berra
15. Alex Ferguson
16. Estonia
17. Colin Stein
18. Sweden
19. 1977
20. 1998

MEDIUM

Quiz 61: Fill in the Blank

Identify who or what is missing from the following sequences:

1. Sam Allardyce, _____, Gary Megson, Owen Coyle

2. Uruguay, Italy, Italy, Uruguay, _____

3. _____, Joe Royle, Kevin Keegan, Stuart Pearce

4. Manchester City, Mexico, Ivory Coast, _____

5. Stade de Reims, Fiorentina, AC Milan, Stade de Reims, _____

6. Kevin Keegan, _____, Alan Shearer, Chris Hughton, Alan Pardew

7. Borussia Mönchengladbach, Club Brugge, Real Madrid, Roma, _____

8. Argentina, Czechoslovakia, Hungary, _____

9. Niall Quinn, Roy Keane, _____, Steve Bruce, Martin O'Neill

10. Mexico, West Germany, Argentina, Spain, _____

11. Milk, Littlewoods, _____, Coca Cola, Worthington

12. Grzegorz Lato, Mario Kempes, Paolo Rossi, Gary Lineker, _____

13. West Germany, France, Holland, _____, Germany

14. _____, Axa, E.On, Budweiser

15. Manchester United, Everton, Manchester United, Liverpool, _____

16. Leyland Daf, Autoglass, Auto Windscreens, _____, Johnstone's Paints

17. West Ham, Manchester United, _____, Everton, Portsmouth

18. Tommy Docherty, _____, Ron Atkinson, Alex Ferguson

19. Moscow, Rome, Madrid, London, _____

20. Paul Sturrock, Brian Laws, _____, Gary Megson, Dave Jones

MEDIUM

Answers to Quiz 60: Pot Luck

1. Australian
2. Preston North End
3. France
4. Celtic Park
5. Coventry City
6. Glentoran
7. Bobby Moore
8. Bury
9. Falkirk and Forfar
10. Richard Kingson
11. Robert Earnshaw, Dean Saunders, Gary Speed and Mark Hughes
12. Bill Shankly
13. Rob Jones
14. John Ruddy
15. Oxford United
16. Liverpool and Arsenal
17. Hibernian
18. Marco van Basten
19. Dugouts
20. Birmingham City

Quiz 62: Pot Luck

1. Which three Scots have won the FA Premier League Manager of the Season award?

2. Which team were promoted to the Football League after winning the 2012 conference play off final?

3. Who scored goals against three different goalkeepers in West Ham's 8-1 thumping of Newcastle in 1986?

4. Can you name the eight London clubs that competed in the top flight in 1989/90?

5. Mark Hughes played abroad at Barcelona and what other club?

6. Which Scottish Premier League club was named after an English rugby union team?

7. Which team has won the most Northern Ireland championships?

8. Rombo di Tuono (Roar of Thunder) was the nickname of which Italian striker?

9. Which England cricketer was unimpressed with the management at Chelsea, tweeting, 'Who is the muppet coaching Chelsea??? AVB??? Hmmm!! 25yrs for Ferguson, hopefully not even 6 months for this AVB geezer!'?

10. Before Spain in 2008, who were the last European Championship winners to go through the tournament unbeaten?

11. Which striker, who had spells at Arsenal and West Ham, won the Golden Boot at the 1998 World Cup?

12. Who were the original hosts of TV's Soccer AM?

13. Which team wore a brown away kit in the 1970s?

14. In addition to Tottenham, Ossie Ardiles played for what other three English clubs?

15. Which three England captains played for Scunthorpe United?

16. Which player has league and cup winner's medals in England, Scotland and Spain and also won the Champions League?

17. Up to 2012, five players have played for Manchester United and Barcelona. Can you name them?

18. Which Wolves and Stoke defender, noted for his glorious afro, was born in Germany and played international football for Wales?

Answers to Quiz 61: Fill in the Blank

1. Sammy Lee
(Bolton managers)

2. West Germany (first five
World Cup winners)

3. Frank Clark
(Manchester City managers)

4. Leicester City
(teams managed by
Sven-Göran Eriksson)

5. Eintracht Frankfurt
(first five European Cup
runners-up)

6. Joe Kinnear
(Newcastle managers)

7. AC Milan (teams defeated
by Liverpool in the
European Cup final)

8. Brazil (first four losing
World Cup finalists)

9. Ricky Sbragia
(Sunderland managers)

10. Mexico (World Cup hosts
1970 to 1986)

11. Rumbelows
(League Cup sponsors)

12. Salvatore Schillaci
(World Cup Golden Boot
winners)

13. Denmark
(European Championship
winners 1980 to 1996)

14. Littlewoods
(FA Cup sponsors)

15. Coventry City
(FA Cup winners 1983-1987)

16. LDV Vans (sponsors of the
Football League Trophy)

17. Cardiff City
(FA Cup final runners-up
2007 to 2010)

18. Dave Sexton (Manchester
United managers)

19. Munich
(Champions League final
cities 2008 to 2012)

20. Alan Irvine (Sheffield
Wednesday managers)

MEDIUM

Quiz 63: Milestones

1. What was used for the first time at Nottingham Forest's ground in 1878?

2. Who was the first man to win the European Footballer of the Year award?

3. What cricket ground hosted England's first ever home international?

4. Who, in 2006, became the first third-flight team to reach the Scottish Cup final?

5. After a 14-year career, who played his final match against Yugoslavia on 18 July 1971?

6. Who were the first British team to win two European trophies?

7. Which German scored the first penalty in a World Cup final?

8. The first double sending-off at Wembley happened in what game, in which year?

9. What did West Brom's Dennis Clarke do in 1968 that nobody had done before?

10. Who, in 1978 and 1979, became the first player to play in different FA Cup winning teams in successive seasons?

11. What is the only Football League club to both score and concede 100 goals in the same season?

12. Who was the first German to play in an FA Cup final?

13. In 1987/88, Stirling became the first Scottish team to do what?

14. What was the venue for the first European Cup final?

15. The first Englishman to manage a team in the World Cup final was in charge of which country?

16. Who, in 2006, became the first English team to beat Real Madrid at the Bernabeu?

17. The only match between West Germany and East Germany took place at what World Cup? Who won?

18. Which team won the only European Cup that was decided by a replay?

19. Sir Alf Ramsey's last game as England manager came against which opposition?
    a) Poland
    b) Portugal
    c) Peru

20. In what decade did the white ball first come into official use in English football?
    a) 1940s
    b) 1950s
    c) 1960s

Answers to Quiz 62: Pot Luck

1. Alex Ferguson, Kenny Dalglish and George Burley
2. York City
3. Alvin Martin
4. Tottenham, Arsenal, Chelsea, Wimbledon, QPR, Crystal Palace, Charlton and Millwall
5. Bayern Munich
6. Rangers
7. Linfield
8. Luigi Riva
9. Kevin Pietersen
10. Germany in 1996
11. Davor Suker
12. Helen Chamberlain and Russ Hamilton
13. Coventry City
14. Blackburn, QPR and Swindon Town
15. Kevin Keegan, Ray Clemence and Ian Botham (who played for Scunny and captained the England cricket team)
16. Giovanni van Bronckhorst
17. Mark Hughes, Gerard Piqué, Laurent Blanc, Johan Cruyff and Henrik Larsson
18. George Berry

MEDIUM

Quiz 64: Pot Luck

1. The headquarters of FIFA are in which city?

2. Who were the first team to wear a sponsored shirt in an English league game?

3. St Johnstone are based in which Scottish city?

4. Who is the only person to captain England and manage a team in the European Cup final?

5. Which manager said, 'Football hooligans? Well, there are 92 club chairmen for a start'?

6. Who was the first black English manager in England's top flight?

7. Choccy was the nickname of which Manchester United striker?

8. Marco Materazzi, who was on the receiving end of Zinedine Zidane's famous head butt, had a brief spell with which English club?

9. Who was Middlesbrough's manager when they won their first major trophy?

10. A group of Italian writers used the name of which England striker as a pseudonym for their novel Q?

11. Which London ground used to have a section known as the Chicken Run?

12. The Glaziers was the former nickname of which English club?

13. Which player-turned-pundit was the first professional footballer to be fined in a criminal court for an on-pitch assault of an opponent?

14. Which European coach responded to accusations that he wore a wig by saying, 'I've heard that before too. Rubbish. You're welcome to tug on it'?

15. What was former Manchester City winger Kiki Musampa's nickname?

16. Roy Keane joined Nottingham Forest from which Irish club?

17. Afan Lido is a club based in which Welsh town?

18. Zinedine Zidane played for which four clubs?

19. What does Barcelona's nickname Los Culés translate to in English?
    a) The Cabbages
    b) The Onions
    c) The Red Peppers

20. Thomas Ravelli is the most capped player for which country?
    a) Iceland
    b) Norway
    c) Sweden

MEDIUM

Answers to Quiz 63: Milestones

1. A referee's whistle
2. Stanley Matthews
3. The Oval
4. Gretna
5. Pele
6. Tottenham
7. Paul Breitner
8. 1974 Charity Shield
9. Appear as a substitute in an FA Cup final
10. Brian Talbot
11. Manchester City in 1957/58
12. Bert Trautmann
13. Play on a plastic pitch
14. Parc des Princes in Paris
15. Sweden (George Raynor)
16. Arsenal
17. 1974 East Germany won 1-0
18. Bayern Munich
19. Portugal
20. 1950s

Quiz 65: Around the British Isles

1. Who is the leading goal-scorer in Welsh Premier League history?

2. Which successful Football League boss started his managerial career with Bangor City?

3. What Welsh Premier League side was formerly known as Total Network Solutions F.C.?

4. Which Irish club is nicknamed The Candystripes?

5. What is the name of the trophy awarded to the winners of the IFA Premiership?

6. Which team won the League of Ireland Premier Division in 2010 and 2011?

7. Which team shocked Celtic in the 1995 Scottish League Cup final?

8. Which Irish team play their home games at The Oval?

9. Former Wolves, Tranmere, Stockport and Burnley midfielder Paul Cook left which Irish club to take the manager's job at Accrington Stanley?

10. Which Northern Irish team reached the quarterfinal of the 1966/67 European Cup?

11. Which two Highland League clubs were admitted to the Scottish Football League in 2001/02?

12. Which League of Ireland Premier Division team play at Oriel Park?

13. Which Scottish club is nicknamed The Ton?

14. Éamon Zayed, the leading scorer in the 2011 League of Ireland Premier Division, plays international football for which country?

15. Which former English Football League club call Aggborough home?

16. Who were the first sponsors of the League of Ireland Premier Division?

17. Which Scottish club play at New Douglas Park?

18. Which former Tottenham and Wolves midfielder enjoyed a spell at Shamrock Rovers in 2011?

19. How many teams make up the IFA Premiership?
    a) 10
    b) 12
    c) 14

20. Stebonheath Park is the home ground of which Welsh club?
    a) Llanelli
    b) Rhyl
    c) Cwmbran Town

MEDIUM

Answers to Quiz 64: Pot Luck

1. Zurich
2. Liverpool
3. Perth
4. Jimmy Armfield
5. Brian Clough
6. Paul Ince
7. Brian McClair
8. Everton
9. Steve McClaren
10. Luther Blissett
11. Upton Park
12. Crystal Palace
13. Chris Kamara
14. Joachim Löw
15. Chris (Chris Musampa)
16. Cobh Ramblers
17. Port Talbot
18. Cannes, Bordeaux, Juventus and Real Madrid
19. The Cabbages
20. Sweden

Quiz 66: Pot Luck

1. Which Bayern Munich and Germany defender is nicknamed The Magic Dwarf?

2. In February 2011, Andy Carroll and Kenny Dalglish were spotted at what unlikely event?

3. Which Dutch darts fan said, 'A great team never eases off after a good win. In that respect, we can learn from Phil Taylor'?

4. Which Arsenal player broke his arm after being dropped by Tony Adams during the team's 1993 League Cup winning celebrations?

5. Who was the only Wimbledon player to score a hat trick in the Premier League?

6. Who are the five footballers to have won the BBC Sports Personality of the Year award?

7. Jermaine Defoe scored 18 goals in a loan spell at which lower league club?

8. Who is the only European Footballer of the Year to have played in Scotland?

9. Brian Moore's Head Looks Uncannily Like The London Planetarium was a fanzine devoted to which club?

10. What was the name of the 1979 film starring Ian McShane as a boozy footballer for Leicester Forest?

11. What was the former name of The King Baudouin Stadium?

12. Can you name the five clubs that Alan Pardew has managed?

13. Fans of baseball team the Minnesota Twins have reworked the anthem of which English club?

14. Who was the subject of a book subtitled From Hitler Youth to FA Cup Legend?

15. Which League 2 club beat Newcastle 3-1 in the third round of the 2011 FA Cup?

16. Which two teams take part in the A420 derby?

17. Which Dutch player won the Football Writers' Association Player of the Year in 1981?

18. Which defender holds the record for the most Premier League appearances without being capped by England?

19. Former Wimbledon champion Stefan Edberg is a fan of which English club?
    a) Aston Villa
    b) Everton
    c) Leeds United

20. True or false – Spain lost international penalty shoot-outs on the same date, 22 June, in 1986, 1996 and 2002?

Answers to Quiz 65: Around the British Isles

1. Marc Lloyd Williams
2. Nigel Adkins
3. The New Saints
4. Derry City
5. Gibson Cup
6. Shamrock Rovers
7. Raith Rovers
8. Glentoran
9. Sligo Rovers
10. Linfield
11. Peterhead and Elgin City
12. Dundalk
13. Morton
14. Libya
15. Kidderminster Harriers
16. Bord Gáis
17. Hamilton Academical
18. Rohan Ricketts
19. 12
20. Llanelli

MEDIUM

Quiz 67: League Cup

MEDIUM

1. Who did Aston Villa beat in the first League Cup final?

2. Who was the first non-British manager to guide a team to League Cup victory?

3. Which team lost in the final in both 1997 and 1998?

4. Which two teams have won the League Cup and been relegated in the same season?

5. Who were the first team to win a League Cup final after a penalty shoot-out?

6. Which four teams have won the League and the League Cup in the same season?

7. Who did Norwich beat in the 1985 final?

8. Who is the only Spanish manager to have won the League Cup?

9. Who were Birmingham's goalscorers in the 2011 final?

10. Which team won the trophy in 1974 and 1980?

11. Who won the first final at the new Wembley?

12. Which two clubs from the third tier of English football have won the League Cup?

13. Liverpool won the trophy in four consecutive seasons between 1981 and 1984. Who did they beat in the finals?

14. Which team appeared in three finals in four years between 1997 and 2000?

15. Which midfielder scored a 40-yard spectacular in Crystal Palace's surprise quarterfinal win over Manchester United in 2011?

16. Who scored 12 League Cup goals for Tottenham in the 1986/87 season?

17. Which club won the first League Cup final staged at Wembley?

18. Which three players were sent off in the 2006 final?

19. Who did Stoke City beat to win their only League Cup?
    a) Arsenal
    b) Chelsea
    c) West Ham

20. Who was the Aston Villa manager when they lifted the trophy in 1996?
    a) Ron Atkinson
    b) Brian Little
    c) Graham Taylor

MEDIUM

Answers to Quiz 66: Pot Luck

1. Philipp Lahm
2. A Boyzone concert
3. Robin van Persie
4. Steve Morrow
5. Dean Holdsworth
6. Bobby Moore, Paul Gascoigne, Michael Owen, David Beckham and Ryan Giggs
7. Bournemouth
8. George Best
9. Gillingham
10. Yesterday's Hero
11. Heysel Stadium
12. Reading, West Ham, Charlton, Southampton and Newcastle
13. Leeds United's Marching On Together
14. Bert Trautmann
15. Stevenage
16. Swindon Town and Oxford United
17. Frans Thijssen
18. Chris Perry
19. Leeds United
20. True

DIFFICULT QUIZZES

Quiz 68: Pot Luck

1. The main characters in TV drama New Tricks are named after stands at which football club?
2. Why was youngster Jacob Mellis sacked by Chelsea in 2012?
3. In 2008, 38-year-old Ivica Vastic became the oldest scorer in the history of the European Championship finals. What country was he playing for?
4. Who scored in all four divisions of the old Football League and in the Premier League?
5. Which football club was also one of England legend Bobby Moore's middle names?
6. While at Newcastle, Andy Carroll had a loan spell at which club?
7. Which striker, whose clubs included Reading, Cardiff and Mansfield, served in the Falklands War?
8. Why was the kick-off of Liverpool's 2001 UEFA Cup semi-final against Barcelona delayed for ten minutes?
9. Which football teams played in the first televised match?
10. Which three English Football League teams have all the vowels in their name?
11. Which member of the 1986 England World Cup squad owns the shirt worn by Diego Maradona in the game?
12. What is the only English football team whose name is made up of 'vowels'?
13. The Ali Sami Yen was the long-time stadium of which European club?
14. When was the last time clubs starting with the same letter won the top two divisions in England?
15. Which former Home Secretary went on to become the chairman of Celtic?
16. Tom Finney spent all of his career in England with Preston but also had a short spell with which Irish club?
17. Which Dutch player said, 'All Nottingham has is Robin Hood…and he's dead'?

18. Which club's 106-year spell in the Football League ended after relegation at the end of the 2010/11 season?

19. How many nationalities took part in the 2011/12 Premier League season?
    a) 48
    b) 58
    c) 68

20. After retiring from football, Neil Webb, Micky Gynn and Peter Bonetti had what job?
    a) chef
    b) fireman
    c) postman

Answers to Quiz 100: Pot Luck

1. Oleg Salenko against Cameroon in 1994
2. Germany and Spain
3. Didier Drogba, Thierry Henry, Paul Scholes, Ryan Giggs, Matthew Le Tissier
4. Peter Beardsley and David Johnson
5. Manucho
6. John Hendrie, Gordon Strachan, Kevin Gallagher, Duncan Ferguson, Gary McAllister
7. Sporting Lisbon
8. Darius Vassell
9. Cliftonville
10. Joe Mercer, Bill Nicholson, Don Revie, Sir Alex Ferguson, George Graham, Jose Mourinho and Kenny Dalglish
11. Boca Juniors
12. Garrincha
13. Northern Ireland's David Healy with 13
14. Clint Dempsey
15. Egypt
16. United beat Liga Deportiva Universitaria de Quito from Ecuador
17. He was accused of sprinkling black magic charms on the pitch
18. Copa America
19. 22
20. Stockport County

DIFFICULT

Quiz 69: Books

Identify the footballer who is the subject of each of the following books:

1. Football: It's A Minging Life

2. Mr Unbelievable

3. How Not To Be A Professional Footballer

4. I'm Not Really Here

5. No Smoke, No Fire

6. The Good, The Mad and The Ugly

7. Boozing, Betting & Brawling – A Footballer's Life

8. Tackling My Demons

9. Who Ate All The Pies?

10. Takenote!

11. Steak... Diana Ross: Diary of a Football Nobody

12. Addicted

13. Who's the B*****d in the Black?: Confessions of a Premiership Referee

14. Back From The Brink

15. Super Tramp: My Autobiography

16. Left Field: A Footballer Apart

17. Walking On Water

18. One Hump Or Two?

19. Hard Man: Hard Game

20. First Among Unequals

Answers to Quiz 68: Pot Luck

1. West Bromwich Albion
2. He set off a smoke bomb at the training ground
3. Austria
4. Alan Cork
5. Chelsea
6. Preston North End
7. Phil Stant
8. They had to wait for the end of an EastEnders special
9. Arsenal v Arsenal Reserves in 1937
10. Hartlepool United, Rotherham United and Torquay United
11. Steve Hodge
12. Wolves
13. Galatasaray
14. 1990 Liverpool and Leeds
15. John Reid
16. Distillery
17. Bryan Roy
18. Stockport County
19. 68
20. Postman

DIFFICULT

143

Quiz 70: Pot Luck

1. True or false – football is mentioned in Shakespeare's play Hamlet?

2. Which Scottish striker has scored five goals in a game against Dundee United on two occasions?

3. Which Aston Villa defender scored all four goals in his side's 2-2 draw with Leicester in 1976?

4. What was strange about Darren Bent's goal for Sunderland against Liverpool in 2009?

5. The smallest crowd for a full England international at Wembley was 15,628 in 1989. Who were England's opponents that day?

6. Pope John Paul II attended a youth rally at which football league ground on his 1982 visit to Britain?

7. Arsenal won their last game at Highbury 4-2. Who were their opponents?

8. Which two European teams contest the Derby of Eternal Enemies?

9. Hollywood superstar Hugh Jackman is a fan of which English club?

10. Who was the first non-Basque to play for Real Sociedad, scoring 40 goals in 63 games between 1989 and 1991?

11. Which footballer had a top 40 hit in 1979 with Head Over Heels?

12. While at Leeds United, James Milner enjoyed a brief spell on loan at which club?

13. Salubritas et Industria is the motto of which Football League club?

14. What is the lowest number of Premier League points a team has gained and still managed to avoid relegation?

15. Who scored four goals coming off the bench against Nottingham Forest in February 1999?

Answers - page 147

16. Which legendary player would slap his goalkeeper in the stomach then spit chewing gum into the opponent's half before a game?

17. Can you name six players who won England caps while at five different clubs?

18. Who scored more goals in the Premier League – Les Ferdinand or Teddy Sheringham?

19. Who was the leading English Premier League goalscorer in 2010/11?
    a) Darren Bent
    b) Wayne Rooney
    c) Andy Carroll

20. How many teams took part in the 2011/12 FA Cup?
    a) 376
    b) 637
    c) 763

Answers to Quiz 69: Books

1. Rick Holden
2. Chris Kamara
3. Paul Merson
4. Paul Lake
5. Dave Jones
6. Andy Morrison
7. Mel Sterland
8. Stan Collymore
9. Mick Quinn
10. Darren Anderton
11. Dave McVay
12. Tony Adams
13. Jeff Winter
14. Paul McGrath
15. John Robertson
16. Graeme Le Saux
17. Brian Clough
18. Frank Worthington
19. Larry Lloyd
20. Viv Anderson

DIFFICULT

Quiz 71: Goalkeepers

1. Which goalkeeper was appointed Sheriff of Norwich in 2002?
2. Peter Shilton is one of two goalkeepers to have won the PFA Player of the Year award. Who is the other?
3. Which former Premier League goalkeeper was once an intern at NASA and has a degree in mechanical engineering?
4. Who is the only goalkeeper to win the European Footballer of the Year award?
5. Who was the first goalkeeper to score in a Premier League game?
6. David Seaman played for which five English league clubs?
7. Former Portsmouth, Sunderland, Derby, Arsenal and Watford keeper Mart Poom won 120 caps for which country?
8. What was the name of the goalkeeper who scored eight goals in 74 appearances for Paraguay?
9. Who, in 2009, became the first England goalkeeper to be sent off?
10. What was the name of Reading's wig-wearing, Bulgarian stopper?
11. How many goalkeepers have captained their team to World Cup victory?
12. Which former top-flight goalkeeper played Minor Counties cricket for Shropshire in 1983 and 1984?
13. Peter Shilton made his record-breaking 1,000th league appearance while playing for which club?
14. Australian keeper Mark Schwarzer started his career in England with which club?
15. Gordon Banks made his Football League debut with which club?
16. At 39 years and 321 days, who in 2010 became the oldest player to make his World Cup finals debut?

17. Primrose is the middle name of which goalkeeper-turned-broadcaster?

18. Who was the second goalkeeper to save a penalty in a Wembley FA Cup final?

19. Between 1994 and 2006, the best goalkeeper at the World Cup received what award?
    a) Banks Award
    b) Yashin Award
    c) Zoff Award

20. What nationality is Bolton Wanderers goalkeeper Adam Bogdan?
    a) Bulgarian
    b) Hungarian
    c) Romanian

Answers to Quiz 70: Pot Luck

1. False - but it is mentioned in King Lear and The Comedy of Errors
2. Kris Boyd
3. Chris Nicholl
4. It was deflected in by a beach ball
5. Chile
6. Cardiff City's Ninian Park
7. Wigan Athletic
8. Olympiacos and Panathinaikos
9. Norwich City
10. John Aldridge
11. Kevin Keegan
12. Swindon Town
13. Swindon Town
14. 34 by West Bromwich Albion in 2004/05
15. Ole Gunnar Solskjaer
16. Johann Cruyff
17. Peter Shilton, David Platt, David James, Emile Heskey, Scott Parker and Dave Watson
18. Les Ferdinand with 149 (Sheringham scored 147)
19. Darren Bent
20. 763

DIFFICULT

Quiz 72: Pot Luck

1. Who is the only winning captain to score a goal in the World Cup final?

2. Cobi Jones, America's most capped player, had a spell at which English club?

3. What English town is also the middle name of Manchester City defender Micah Richards?

4. Who is England's most capped player at Under-21 level?

5. Which Scottish footballer played Robert Duvall's son in-law in the 2001 film A Shot At Glory?

6. What was the first club in England to change the name of its ground in a naming rights sponsorship deal?

7. Which Tottenham goalkeeper was the Premier League's first substitute?

8. Nikodem is the middle name of which England defender?

9. Paul Gascoigne's last Football League appearance was with which club?

10. Who, in 1980, was the first Liverpool player to win the PFA Footballer of the Year award?

11. What is the smallest country by size and population to qualify for the World Cup finals?

12. Which three teams have won all four divisions in English football?

13. Which tough-tackling Wolves and Sunderland defender has made a name for himself off the pitch as an artist?

14. George Best scored 20 league goals in a season for Manchester United in 1967/68 but who was the next United player to manage that feat?

15. Which League 2 side knocked Liverpool out of the League Cup in 2010 after winning a penalty shoot-out at Anfield?

16. In 2008, which player finished runner-up in the Premier League, Champions League, League Cup and European Championship?

17. True or false – James Herriot, the creator of All Creatures Great and Small, took his pen name from a Birmingham City goalkeeper?

18. Which defender netted after just 45 seconds in the 2005 League Cup final between Chelsea and Liverpool?

19. What was unique about Bolton's 1958 FA Cup-winning side?
    a) they were all Scottish
    b) they were all over 30
    c) none of them cost the club a transfer fee

20. In what year did the first Charity Shield match take place?
    a) 1908
    b) 1918
    c) 1928

Answers to Quiz 71: Goalkeepers

1. Bryan Gunn
2. Pat Jennings
3. Shaka Hislop
4. Lev Yashin
5. Peter Schmeichel
6. Peterborough United, Birmingham City, QPR, Arsenal and Manchester City
7. Estonia
8. José Luis Chilavert
9. Robert Green
10. Borislav 'Bobby' Mihailov
11. Three (Gianpiero Combi in 1934, Dino Zoff 1982 and Iker Casillas 2010)
12. Steve Ogrizovic
13. Leyton Orient
14. Bradford City
15. Chesterfield
16. David James
17. Bob Wilson
18. Mark Crossley
19. Yashin Award
20. Hungarian

DIFFICULT

Quiz 73: FA Cup

1. Who are the only non-league team to win the FA Cup?

2. Kevin Moran was the first player sent off in an FA Cup final but who was the second?

3. Which Scotsman scored at both ends in the 1981 FA Cup final?

4. Who was the manager of the Bournemouth side that dumped Manchester United out of the Cup in 1984?

5. Which former Gibraltar international cricketer scored a hat trick for non-league Woking to knock West Brom out of the Cup in 1991?

6. The first FA Cup final was held at which ground?

7. Ronnie Radford famously scored for Hereford against Newcastle in 1972 but which player scored the winning goal?

8. Which non-league club knocked top-flight Birmingham City out of the competition in 1986?

9. Who is the only player to score a hat trick in an FA Cup final staged at Wembley?

10. Which team won the FA Cup in 1939 and then held the trophy until 1946?

11. Which third-flight team reached the semifinal in 1997?

12. How did Southampton's Paul Jones make history in the 2003 final?

13. What was used for the first, and so far only time, in the 1973 FA Cup final?

14. Which team won the first FA Cup final hosted at the Millennium Stadium?

15. Who was the only player to win four FA Cup winner's medals at the old Wembley?

16. Which team has lost all four of its FA Cup final appearances, most recently in 1969?

17. Who was the man of the match in the 2012 FA Cup final?

18. Who is the only player to have scored in four FA Cup finals?

19. What was unique about Manchester United's 1948 win?
    a) they played every match bar the final at home
    b) they played every match bar the final away
    c) they played top-flight opposition in every round

20. Which team won the first ever FA Cup final?
    a) Royal Engineers
    b) Old Etonians
    c) Wanderers

Answers to Quiz 72: Pot Luck

1. Carlos Alberto
2. Coventry City
3. Lincoln
4. James Milner with 46
5. Ally McCoist
6. Scarborough – McCain Stadium
7. Erik Thorstvedt
8. Phil Jagielka
9. Boston United
10. Terry McDermott
11. Trinidad and Tobago
12. Wolves, Burnley and Preston
13. Jody Craddock
14. Brian McClair
15. Northampton Town
16. Michael Ballack
17. True
18. Jon Arne Riise
19. None of them cost the club a transfer fee
20. 1908

DIFFICULT

Quiz 74: Pot Luck

1. Which Scottish club have twice reached the FA Cup final?

2. Who, in March 2012, became the first Icelandic player to be named Premier League Player of the Month?

3. During his lengthy career, Peter Shilton played over 100 games for five different clubs. Which five?

4. Gary Lineker scored six of England's seven goals at the 1986 World Cup. Who scored the other?

5. Who were England's three goalscorers in the 2010 World Cup in South Africa?

6. Which former Stockport, Oxford and Birmingham striker is now a Vancouver-based policeman?

7. Eric Cantona joined Leeds United from which French club?

8. What is the fewest number of points a team has won the Premier League with?

9. Which Liverpool player is a qualified tattoo artist?

10. Which four Tottenham players have won the PFA Players' Player of the Year award?

11. Who, in 1994, became the first player to be sent off in a League Cup final?

12. Which legendary player has finished runner-up in 17 competitions including three times in Serie A, three Champions League finals, one World Cup and one European Championship?

13. Which goalkeeper played in all four divisions in 1986/87?

14. Which outfield player played in all four divisions in 2000/01?

15. Who are the three Ukrainians to have been named European Footballer of the Year?

16. Who was the first English player to be sold for £5m?

17. True or false – Manchester United once played a home league game at Anfield?

18. The highest attendance at a bottom tier game in England was for a game at what ground?

19. Manchester United set the record for the most consecutive clean sheets in 2008/09. How many games did they go without conceding a goal?
    a) 12
    b) 13
    c) 14

20. In what year was the Football Association founded?
    a) 1863
    b) 1873
    c) 1883

Answers to Quiz 73: FA Cup

1. Tottenham Hotspur (in 1901)
2. Jose Antonio Reyes
3. Tommy Hutchison
4. Harry Redknapp
5. Tim Buzaglo
6. The Oval
7. Ricky George
8. Altrincham
9. Stan Mortensen
10. Portsmouth
11. Chesterfield
12. He was the first goalkeeper to come off the bench in an FA Cup final
13. An orange ball
14. Liverpool
15. Mark Hughes
16. Leicester City
17. Juan Mata
18. Didier Drogba
19. They played top-flight opposition in every round
20. Wanderers

DIFFICULT

Quiz 75: England

1. Fabio Capello was in charge of England for 42 matches. How many of them did they lose?

2. Four players wore the captain's armband during England's 2003 game against Serbia and Montenegro. Can you name them?

3. Who scored the goals in England's famous 2-0 win over Brazil in Rio in 1984?

4. Which Preston striker scored on his England debut in 2007?

5. Who is the only player to win a full England cap while playing at Celtic?

6. Which former England striker was born in French Guiana?

7. Four England players have won caps while at German clubs. Can you name them?

8. Who scored just 16 seconds after coming on as a sub in England's World Cup qualifier against Greece in 2001?

9. Which four players started a game for England in the 1966 World Cup but didn't play in the final?

10. Who is the only player to win an England cap while at a Turkish club?

11. Which club has provided the most players to the England team?

12. Who did England beat 3-0 in Sven-Göran Eriksson's first match in charge?

13. Both Billy Wright and Bobby Moore captained England in the same number of matches. How many?

14. Who won his first three England caps while playing at three different clubs?

15. Since 1980, nine players have played for England while at Italian clubs. Can you name the nine?

16. A different manager was in charge for which player's first four international appearances?

17. Which much-travelled striker scored on his one and only England appearance against Australia in 2003?

18. Who won his second cap against France in the 1966 World Cup then had to wait over 11 years to win his third?

19. Which non-English club has provided the most England internationals?
    a) Rangers
    b) AC Milan
    c) Real Madrid

20. How old was Bobby Moore when he captained England for the first time?
    a) 22
    b) 23
    c) 24

Answers to Quiz 74: Pot Luck

1. Queen's Park
2. Gylfi Sigurdsson
3. Leicester City, Stoke City, Nottingham Forest, Southampton and Derby County
4. Peter Beardsley
5. Steven Gerrard, Jermain Defoe and Matthew Upson
6. Kevin Francis
7. Nîmes
8. 75 by Manchester United in 1996/97
9. Daniel Agger
10. Pat Jennings, Clive Allen, David Ginola and Gareth Bale
11. Andrei Kanchelskis
12. Paolo Maldini
13. Eric Nixon
14. Tony Cottee
15. Oleg Blokhin, Igor Belanov and Andriy Shevchenko
16. David Platt
17. True (in 1971 United were banned from playing their first two home games at Old Trafford)
18. Crystal Palace's Selhurst Park
19. 14
20. 1863

DIFFICULT

Quiz 76: Pot Luck

1. Who has scored hat tricks for Liverpool in the Premier League, FA Cup and Champions League?

2. Which manager, who cites Kandinsky as his favourite painter, is believed to have an art collection worth £10m?

3. Which two South American countries did England meet in the 2006 World Cup?

4. Steve McClaren had a brief spell managing which German club?

5. How many teams managed to retain the European Cup Winners' Cup?

6. True or false – Brazil used to wear white shirts and only changed to yellow after losing the 1950 World Cup final?

7. Wimbledon champion Bjorn Borg is a huge fan of which London club?

8. Which footballer had a role in the 2006 film Basic Instinct 2?

9. Rosenkrands is the middle name of which Premier League striker?

10. Who, in 2011, became the first player to win the League Cup final man of the match award twice?

11. The Bully Wee is the nickname of which Scottish club?

12. Which defender, whose surname is a capital city, enjoyed spells at Crystal Palace, Wolves, Rangers and Millwall between 1996 and 2005?

13. Which club, in 1987, became the first to be automatically relegated from the Football League to the Conference?

14. Which member of a famous footballing family took charge of Barnet for the third time in April 2012?

15. Who did Sepp Blatter succeed as FIFA President?

16. Which Ipswich defender won the first PFA Young Player of the Year award in 1974?

17. What country was originally chosen to host the 1986 World Cup but withdrew due to financial problems?

18. How many top-flight teams did Millwall play en route to the 2004 FA Cup final?
    a) 0
    b) 3
    c) 6

19. In what decade was the Charity Shield held at Wembley for the first time?
    a) 1950s
    b) 1960s
    c) 1970s

Answers to Quiz 75: England

1. Six
2. Michael Owen, Jamie Carragher, Emile Heskey and Phil Neville
3. John Barnes and Mark Hateley
4. David Nugent
5. Alan Thompson
6. Cyrille Regis
7. Kevin Keegan (Hamburg), Dave Watson (Werder Bremen), Tony Woodcock (FC Cologne), Owen Hargreaves (Bayern Munich)
8. Teddy Sheringham
9. Ian Callaghan, John Connelly, Jimmy Greaves and Terry Paine
10. Scott Carson
11. Aston Villa
12. Spain
13. 90
14. Scott Parker
15. Trevor Francis, Mark Hateley, Luther Blissett, Ray Wilkins, Gordon Cowans, David Platt, Des Walker, Paul Gascoigne, David Beckham (on loan at AC Milan)
16. Andy Cole
17. Francis Jeffers
18. Ian Callaghan
19. Rangers with 7
20. 22

DIFFICULT

Quiz 77: World Cup

1. Who is the only Scottish player to score in three World Cups?

2. Which team won the World Cup despite losing to their final opponents 8-3 in the group stage?

3. Who did Hungary beat 10-1 in the 1982 World Cup in Spain?

4. What World Cup feat has only been achieved by Bora Milutinovic and Carlos Alberto Parreira?

5. Who are the only two men to have won the World Cup as a player and as a manager?

6. What was the only team to remain unbeaten at the 2010 World Cup in South Africa?

7. How many times has a team wearing red shirts won the World Cup final?

8. Who won the Golden Ball award for the best player of the tournament at the 2010 World Cup?

9. How did Josip Simunic make history in Croatia's match against Australia in 2006?

10. Which two teams took part in the 3rd/4th place play-off at the 2002 World Cup?

11. In what year did the first World Cup penalty shoot-out take place?

12. Which three captains have led their team in two World Cup finals?

13. In 2006, which country was eliminated from the finals without conceding a goal?

14. Who were the only team to lose their World Cup opening match and still go on to win the tournament?

15. Who became the first Central American team to win a World Cup match in Europe after beating Scotland 1-0 in 1990?

16. Which former Portsmouth midfielder is the only man to score for two countries in World Cup finals matches?

17. Who is the only goalkeeper to have been named Player of the Tournament in a World Cup?

18. Which Italian became the first goalkeeper to be sent off in a World Cup match in the Azzurri's match against Norway in 1994?

19. Who were the first African team to take part in the World Cup?
    a) Cameroon
    b) Egypt
    c) Zaire

20. How many teams entered the first World Cup?
    a) 13
    b) 17
    c) 19

Answers to Quiz 76: Pot Luck

1. Yossi Benayoun	11. Clyde
2. Fabio Capello	12. Kevin Muscat
3. Paraguay and Ecuador	13. Lincoln City
4. Wolfsburg	14. Martin Allen
5. None	15. João Havelange
6. True	16. Kevin Beattie
7. Charlton Athletic	17. Colombia
8. Stan Collymore	18. 0
9. Peter Lovenkrands	19. 1970s (1974)
10. Ben Foster	

DIFFICULT

Quiz 78: Pot Luck

1. Which goalkeeper scored his first Premier League goal against Bolton in January 2012?
2. Who were the last team to win second- and top-flight titles in consecutive seasons?
3. Who did Everton beat in the final of the 1985 European Cup Winners' Cup?
4. Who are the only two managers to have steered teams to victory in the World Cup and the Champions League?
5. Which England international played against Liverpool in both an FA Cup final and a European Cup final?
6. Who is the only player to be the English top flight's leading scorer with three different clubs?
7. Which Southampton defender scored a record-setting three Premier League own goals in the 2004/05 season?
8. QPR were forced to play their home 1984/85 UEFA Cup games away from Loftus Road. Where did they play and why?
9. What record did Millwall's Curtis Weston set in the 2004 FA Cup final?
10. Who is the only Ipswich Town player to win the PFA Players' Player of the Year award?
11. Who is the only Dane to have won the European Footballer of the Year award?
12. The Loons is the nickname of which Scottish club?
13. Which two players have won the PFA Player of the Year and Young Player of the Year awards in the same season?
14. Jack Wilshere missed the whole of the 2011/12 season after picking up an injury against which American team?
15. Which Italian defender was given an eight match ban after elbowing Spain's Luis Enrique in the face in the 1994 World Cup?
16. Who is the only Englishman to win the prestigious Golden Shoe award given to Europe's number one marksman?

17. Who scored the winning goal in Italy's first win over England in England in 1973?

18. Which FA Cup giant-killer was a part owner of Earth Summit, the horse that won the 1998 Grand National?

19. Which superstitious England World Cup winner insisted on being the last player in the dressing room to put his shorts on before kick-off?
    a) Bobby Charlton
    b) Bobby Moore
    c) Nobby Stiles

20. What is the most home goals scored by a team in a Premier League season?
    a) 60
    b) 64
    c) 68

Answers to Quiz 77: World Cup

1. Joe Jordan
2. West Germany over Hungary in 1954
3. El Salvador
4. They've coached five different countries at World Cups
5. Franz Beckenbauer and Mario Zagalo
6. New Zealand
7. Once. England in 1966. Spain wore blue in 2010
8. Diego Forlan
9. He received three yellow cards from referee Graham Poll
10. Turkey and South Korea
11. 1982
12. Diego Maradona, Dunga and Karl-Heinz Rummenigge
13. Switzerland
14. Spain in 2010
15. Costa Rica
16. Robert Prosinecki
17. Oliver Kahn in 2002
18. Gianluca Pagliuca
19. Egypt in 1934
20. 13

DIFFICULT

Quiz 79: Wembley

1. Who were the first national team from outside the British Isles to play a full international against England at Wembley?

2. Which two teams were involved in the first FA Cup final replay at Wembley?

3. The Queen has handed out two international trophies at Wembley. The first was to Bobby Moore in 1966. Who received the second?

4. Which centre half scored the last international goal for England at the old Wembley?

5. Which centre half scored the first full international goal at the new Wembley?

6. What is the capacity of Wembley Stadium?

7. Who was the first England player to be sent off in an international at Wembley?

8. In 1991, who became the first African team to play an international at Wembley?

9. Which player holds the record for the most appearances at Wembley?

10. What was the original name of Wembley Stadium?

11. Which Premier League striker scored in his first seven appearances at Wembley?

12. Which monarch opened Wembley in 1924?

13. What was special about Paul Tait's winner for Birmingham in the 1995 Auto Windscreens Shield?

14. In 1989, which team became the first to win two Wembley finals in the same season?

15. In what decade were floodlights first used at Wembley?

16. Which Scot scored a hat trick for Chelsea against Manchester City in the 1985 Full Members Cup?

17. Who is England's leading international goalscorer at Wembley?

18. There is a statue of which former England legend at the end of Wembley Way?

19. Which Italian club won the Cup Winners' Cup at Wembley in 1993?
    a) AC Milan
    b) Parma
    c) Torino

20. How many steps led to the Royal Box at the old Wembley?
    a) 29
    b) 39
    c) 49

Answers to Quiz 78: Pot Luck

1. Tim Howard
2. Ipswich Town in 1960/61 and 1961/62
3. Rapid Vienna
4. Vicente del Bosque and Marcello Lippi
5. Laurie Cunningham
6. Gary Lineker (Leicester, Everton and Tottenham)
7. Andreas Jakobsson
8. Highbury as UEFA wouldn't allow games to be played on artificial pitches
9. He was the youngest player to take part in an FA Cup final
10. John Wark
11. Allan Simonsen
12. Forfar Athletic
13. Andy Gray and Cristiano Ronaldo
14. New York Red Bulls
15. Mauro Tassotti
16. Kevin Phillips
17. Fabio Capello
18. Ricky George
19. Bobby Moore
20. 68 by Chelsea in 2009/10

DIFFICULT

Quiz 80: Pot Luck

1. What was unusual about Tottenham's second goal in the 1967 Charity Shield?

2. Who is the only man to lose a World Cup final as a player and as a manager?

3. Alan Shearer scored five goals in a single game in 1999 against which Premier League club?

4. In what decade was football's maximum wage abolished?

5. True or false – QPR originally wore red and white hoops?

6. Which footballer appeared on reality TV show Celebrity Love Island?

7. Who was the first player to score two penalties in an FA Cup final?

8. Who was the interim England manager between the reigns of Alf Ramsey and Don Revie?

9. Which four French players have a full set of World Cup, European Championship and Champions League winner's medals?

10. What is the only country to have won the World Cup and have one of its clubs win the European Cup in the same year?

11. De Kuip is the home ground of which European club?

12. The 2006 football film Offside is about a World Cup qualifying match in which Asian country?

13. In 2010, which player won a domestic league and cup double and the Champions League as well a being a runner-up in the World Cup?

14. Peter Crouch scored a hat trick for England in 2006 against which country?

15. Who played Peter Taylor in the film The Damned United?

16. Which Premier League defender lists Mozart, meditation and bungee jumping among his hobbies?

17. The fastest goal in World Cup qualifying history was scored

by Davide Gaultieri. Who was he playing for and who were the opposition?

18. Which player, who later became a manager, scored four goals on his Spurs debut in Tottenham's 9-0 drubbing of Bristol Rovers in 1977?

19. The Other Final was a 2003 documentary about a game between the two lowest-ranked national teams in the world. Montserrat was one team, who were their Asian opponents?
    a) Bahrain
    b) Bhutan
    c) Brunei

20. Which team has lost the most FA Cup finals?
    a) Everton
    b) Leicester
    c) Manchester United

Answers to Quiz 79: Wembley

1. Argentina in 1951
2. Tottenham and Manchester City in 1981
3. Jurgen Klinsmann in 1996
4. Tony Adams
5. John Terry
6. 90,000
7. Paul Scholes
8. Cameroon
9. Tony Adams
10. The Empire Stadium
11. Didier Drogba
12. King George V
13. It was the first Wembley final decided by a sudden death goal
14. Nottingham Forest in the League Cup and Simod Cup
15. 1950s
16. David Speedie
17. Bobby Charlton
18. Bobby Moore
19. Parma
20. 39

DIFFICULT

Quiz 81: European Championship

1. Who replaced the substituted Gary Lineker in his last England appearance at Euro 92?

2. Which city hosted the final of Euro 2008?

3. Two countries made their European Championship debut in 2008. Can you name them?

4. Which two England players missed penalties in the 2004 shoot-out loss to Portugal?

5. What nationality was the coach who steered Greece to victory in 2004?

6. Four sets of brothers played in Euro 2000. Can you name them?

7. Who, in 1996, became the first player to score a Golden Goal in a major final?

8. Who were the two losing semifinalists at Euro 2008?

9. Which Dutch goalkeeper saved a penalty in the 1988 final against the USSR?

10. Why were the USSR awarded a walkover in their 1960 semi-final against Spain?

11. Which country defeated England in the 1968 semifinal?

12. Who was the only Englishman named in the Euro 2004 Team of the Tournament?

13. Whose cheekily chipped penalty for Czechoslovakia condemned West Germany to a rare shoot-out defeat in the 1976 final?

14. Who did West Germany beat in the 1980 final?

15. Who was the first man to win the European Championships as both a player and manager?

16. Which country appeared in the final of three of the first four European Championships?

17. Before their group win over Scotland in 1996, in what year had England last won a European Championship match?

18. Who scored the decisive penalty in Spain's 2008 quarter-final shoot-out win over Italy despite never having taken a penalty before?

19. What was unusual about Italy's 1968 semifinal win over the USSR?
    a) The Soviets refused to play so Italy got a bye
    b) The result was decided by the toss of a coin
    c) It was the first European Championship game on a neutral venue

20. How many teams took part in Euro 88?
    a) 8
    b) 16
    c) 24

Answers to Quiz 80: Pot Luck

1. It was scored by goalkeeper Pat Jennings
2. Franz Beckenbauer in 1966 and 1986
3. Sheffield Wednesday
4. 1960s
5. False – but they did wear green and white hoops before adopting blue and white hoops
6. Lee Sharpe
7. Eric Cantona
8. Joe Mercer
9. Marcel Desailly, Bixente Lizarazu, Didier Deschamps and Zinedine Zidane
10. West Germany in 1974 (Bayern Munich)
11. Feyenoord
12. Iran
13. Wesley Sneijder
14. Jamaica
15. Timothy Spall
16. Paul Scharner
17. San Marino and England
18. Colin Lee
19. Bhutan
20. Everton

DIFFICULT

Quiz 82: Pot Luck

1. Who were the only World Cup winners since England in 1966 to win the World Cup final in their change kit?

2. Who is the only Icelandic player to make over 300 Premier League appearances?

3. Which much-relegated striker scored Derby County's last league goal at the Baseball Ground?

4. Which two clubs have won the UEFA Cup and then the European Cup/Champions League the following season?

5. Which two Evertonians have won the PFA Players' Player of the Year award?

6. Who was the only goalkeeper to save a penalty struck by Matthew Le Tissier?

7. Which team finished runners-up in their first season in the top flight in 1982/83?

8. Which private investigator, who was involved in the News of the World phone-hacking scandal, scored AFC Wimbledon's first ever goal?

9. Which German defender likes to prepare for matches by baking cakes?

10. A statue of which Welsh legend can be found outside Swansea City's Liberty Stadium?

11. Darren Anderton was playing for which club when he retired from the game in 2008?

12. Aged just 15 years and 45 days, Reuben Noble-Lazarus made his Championship debut in 2008 for which club?

13. Who holds the record for the most Football League appearances by an outfield player?

14. Which English team were winless for 36 games from September 2007 to September 2008?

15. England players were involved in a row about wearing poppies during a game in 2011. Who were their opponents?

16. Which team won the inaugural second tier of the Football League in 1892/93?

17. What dubious honour connects Andreas Johansson, Keith Gillespie and Dave Kitson?

18. Which Argentine goalkeeper would urinate on the pitch before a penalty shoot-out?

19. John Terry has spent his whole career at Chelsea but enjoyed a brief spell on loan at which club?
    a) Derby County
    b) Nottingham Forest
    c) Preston North End

20. What was unusual about the third-round matches in the 1999/2000 FA Cup?
    a) every Premier League team won
    b) matches took place before Christmas
    c) over half the games were postponed

Answers to Quiz 81: European Championship

1. Alan Smith
2. Vienna
3. Austria and Poland
4. David Beckham and Darius Vassell
5. German
6. Andersson (Sweden), Neville (England), de Boer (Holland), Mpenza (Belgium)
7. Germany's Oliver Bierhoff
8. Russia and Turkey
9. Hans van Breukelen
10. General Franco refused to let the Spain team play in Communist Russia
11. Yugoslavia
12. Wayne Rooney
13. Antonín Panenka
14. Belgium
15. Berti Vogts
16. USSR
17. 1980
18. Cesc Fabregas
19. The result was decided by the toss of a coin
20. 8

DIFFICULT

Quiz 83: Managers part 1

1. Who coached the 1988 Dutch European Championship winning team?

2. Alex Ferguson started his managerial career with which club?

3. Arsene Wenger joined Arsenal from which club?

4. Which three managers have won the European Cup/ Champions League with two different clubs?

5. Bobby Robson won league titles in how many countries?

6. Which manager won the UEFA Cup in 2004 and then the Champions League a year later?

7. Who was the Aston Villa manager for their 1982 European Cup triumph?

8. Which former England manager wore the same 'lucky' dark blue suit on match days for over a decade?

9. Who was the first manager to be sacked in the Premier League era?

10. Which three managers have led teams to promotion on seven occasions (up to 2011/12)?

11. Who was the first manager from outside the British Isles to manage a top-flight English club?

12. Paul Lambert steered Norwich to back-to-back promotions to reach the top-flight. Who was the last manager before him to manage the same feat?

13. Who was the Norwich manager when the Canaries won the League Cup in 1985?

14. Mastermind of England's 1966 World Cup triumph, Alf Ramsey managed Ipswich and what other English club?

15. Alejandro Sabella, who took over as Argentina boss in 2011, had spells as a player with which two English clubs?

16. Who did Ossie Ardiles succeed as Tottenham manager in 1993?

17. Fulham boss Martin Jol had spells at which two English clubs during his playing career?

18. Which manager tried to dampen fan expectations at a new club by saying, 'Look, I'm a coach, I'm not Harry Potter'?

19. Roy Hodgson was sacked as Liverpool manager after how many games in charge?
    a) 21
    b) 31
    c) 41

20. Andre Villas-Boas had a short stint as head coach of which country?
    a) Barbados
    b) Bahamas
    c) British Virgin Islands

Answers to Quiz 82: Pot Luck

1. Spain in 2010
2. Herman Hreidarsson
3. Ashley Ward
4. Liverpool and Porto
5. Peter Reid and Gary Lineker
6. Mark Crossley
7. Watford
8. Glenn Mulcaire
9. Moritz Volz
10. Ivor Allchurch
11. Bournemouth
12. Barnsley
13. Tony Ford with 931
14. Derby County
15. Spain
16. Small Heath
17. They've all been sent off in a Premier League game without touching the ball
18. Sergio Goycochea
19. Nottingham Forest
20. Matches took place before Christmas

DIFFICULT

Quiz 84: Pot Luck

1. Watford beat which third-flight team in the semifinal of the 1984 FA Cup?

2. What was special about the USA's game against Switzerland in Detroit at the 1994 World Cup?

3. Who were the first club to win England's top flight three years in a row?

4. To date, who is the only Austrian to have won the Premier League?

5. Sean Bean starred in which film about a factory worker who finds fame on the football pitch?

6. Glenn Hoddle and Chris Waddle had a number 12 hit in 1987 but what was it called?

7. What is Ricardo Izecson dos Santos Leite better known as?

8. Chris Waddle made his last Football League appearance for which club?

9. Which London club was formed in 1882 by the old boys of Droop Street Board School?

10. Who were the last team from outside the top flight to win the League Cup?

11. Welsh international Ashley Williams made his Football League debut with which club?

12. The highest-ever attendance at Old Trafford was for an FA Cup semifinal between Wolves and which now non-league club?

13. Which five teams have won back to back top-flight titles since the end of the Second World War?

14. The first penalty shoot-out in English domestic football took place in which competition?

15. Who is the only World Cup winner to have played first-class cricket?

16. The first English Football League match under floodlights took place at what ground?

DIFFICULT

17. In 1991, which German became the first winner of FIFA's Player of the Year Award?

18. The manager of which Italian club was sacked in May 2012 after attacking one of his players who had complained about being substituted?

19. Up to and including the 2010 finals, which country has taken part in the most World Cup matches?
    a) Brazil
    b) Germany
    c) Italy

20. Notts County's Lee Hughes missed pre-season training in 2011 because he was suffering from what ailment?
    a) the bends
    b) a snakebite
    c) yellow fever

Answers to Quiz 83: Managers

1. Rinus Michels
2. East Stirlingshire
3. Grampus 8
4. Ernst Happel, Ottmar Hitzfeld and Jose Mourinho
5. Two – Holland and Portugal
6. Rafa Benitez
7. Tony Barton
8. Don Revie
9. Chelsea's Ian Porterfield
10. Neil Warnock, Dave Bassett and Graham Taylor
11. Dr Jozef Venglos with Aston Villa 1990
12. Joe Royle
13. Ken Brown
14. Birmingham City
15. Sheffield United and Leeds United
16. Doug Livermore
17. Coventry City and West Bromwich Albion
18. Jose Mourinho
19. 31
20. British Virgin Islands

DIFFICULT

Quiz 85: Champions League/ European Cup

1. Which teams were involved in the first all-Spanish Champions League final?

2. Which Dutch striker scored for Bayern Munich after just 10.2s against Real Madrid in 2007?

3. Who was the first player to score in the Champions League for five different clubs?

4. What was special about the winning teams from Real Madrid in 1966, Celtic in 1967 and Steaua Bucharest in 1986?

5. In 2002/03, which team lost their first three matches but still progressed through the group stage?

6. Which two cities have provided three Champions League teams in a single season?

7. Which French team lost the first European Cup final?

8. Which Greek club drew all six of their Champions League group games in 2002/03?

9. Wayne Rooney scored a hat trick on his Champions League debut. Who were Manchester United's opponents?

10. Who was the first British player from a British club to score in the Champions League era?

11. Which player has received a red card in the Champions League for three different clubs?

12. Who scored a hat trick for Newcastle against Barcelona in 1997?

13. Who scored the winning penalty in Bayern Munich's 2012 semifinal shoot-out win over Real Madrid?

14. Can you name the five clubs to have won the European Cup/ Champions League in their only appearance in the final?

15. Who was Manchester United's only substitute in the 1968 European Cup final?

16. Who were the first Dutch club to win the European Cup?

17. Which Italian has played in eight European Cup and Champions League finals?

18. Which four Chelsea players were suspended from the 2012 Champions League final?

19. Which Turkish club knocked Manchester City out in the first round of the European Cup in 1968/69?
    a) Besiktas
    b) Fenerbahçe
    c) Galatasaray

20. Since the start of the Premier League, how many different English clubs have qualified for the Champions League?
    a) 8
    b) 9
    c) 10

Answers to Quiz 84: Pot Luck

1. Plymouth Argyle
2. It was the first World Cup match played indoors
3. Huddersfield Town
4. Alex Manninger
5. When Saturday Comes
6. Diamond Lights
7. Kaka
8. Torquay United
9. QPR
10. Sheffield Wednesday in 1991
11. Stockport County
12. Grimsby Town
13. Portsmouth, Manchester United, Wolves, Liverpool and Chelsea
14. The Watney Cup
15. Geoff Hurst
16. Portsmouth's Fratton Park
17. Lothar Matthaus
18. Fiorentina
19. Germany
20. The bends

DIFFICULT

Quiz 86: Pot Luck

1. Who, in 1994, became the first team to win the Charity Shield after a penalty shoot-out?

2. What is the smallest city to host a World Cup final?

3. What is the only English club to win the top flight then get relegated the next season?

4. Who scored a hat trick in QPR's 4-1 win over Manchester United at Old Trafford in 1992?

5. Who, in 2004, became the first German to win a Premier League winner's medal?

6. Which three clubs were founder members of both the Football League and the Premier League?

7. What animal invaded the pitch to disrupt Liverpool's Premier League game against Spurs in February 2012?

8. Which two winners of the old top flight have never played in the Premier League?

9. In 2009, which Scot became the oldest player to make his Premier League debut?

10. Who is the only player to win the FA Cup with both Liverpool and Everton?

11. In 1994, Rashidi Yekini scored which country's first goal at the World Cup finals?

12. Which Fulham defender scored three own goals in the 2010/11 Premier League season?

13. Can you name seven players who have scored in the Premier League for six different clubs?

14. Which superstitious England striker would never take a shot at goal during a warm-up for a game?

15. Manchester City beat which club on penalties in the third tier play-off final in 1999?

16. Which Premier League midfielder has a diploma in fashion design?

17. Who, in 1973, became the first Welsh player to be sent off in an international?

18. What is the most northerly Scottish League team?

19. Why was Hythe's match against Whyteleafe abandoned in March 2012?
    a) the ref's wife went into labour
    b) the ref suffered an allergic reaction to a bee sting
    c) a flock of seagulls invaded the pitch

20. How many steps are there en route to the Royal Box at the rebuilt Wembley Stadium?
    a) 88
    b) 98
    c) 108

Answers to Quiz 85: Champions League/European Cup

1. Real Madrid and Valencia in 2000
2. Roy Makaay
3. Hernan Crespo
4. They all contained only players born in one country
5. Newcastle United
6. London and Athens
7. Stade de Reims
8. AEK Athens
9. Fenerbahçe
10. Mark Hateley (for Rangers)
11. Patrick Vieira
12. Faustino Asprilla
13. Bastian Schweinsteiger
14. Feyenoord, Aston Villa, PSV Eindhoven, Red Star Belgrade and Borussia Dortmund
15. Jimmy Rimmer
16. Feyenoord
17. Paolo Maldini
18. John Terry, Branislav Ivanovic, Ramires and Raul Meireles
19. Fenerbahçe
20. 10

DIFFICULT

Quiz 87: Premier League

1. Which team finished third in the first Premier League season despite conceding more goals than they scored?

2. Who was the first African player to be named Premier League Player of the Month?

3. Which Everton striker scored nine goals in his first eight Premier League games for the club?

4. Which two players have been relegated from the Premier League on five occasions?

5. Who is the only Ukrainian with a Premier League winner's medal?

6. Which Aston Villa midfielder scored the 20,000th Premier League goal?

7. Who were the top-finishing London club in the first Premier League season?

8. Can you name three Russian players who have scored Premier League hat tricks?

9. Which two Bermudans have played in the Premier League?

10. Who was the Southampton manager when the Premier League started?

11. Which five players have notched up 400 Premier League appearances for a single club?

12. Who was the first African to gain a Premier League winner's medal?

13. Which two English managers have led teams to a runners-up finish in the Premier League?

14. Who are the only team to concede 100 goals in a Premier League season?

15. Who are the only team to escape relegation from the Premier League, having been bottom of the table at Christmas?

16. What is the best finish by a team newly promoted to the Premier League?

17. The highest-scoring game in the Premier League was a 7-4 goalfest involving which two clubs?

18. Which team have been relegated from the Premier League the most times?

19. Up to and including the 2011/12 season, how many clubs have appeared in the Premier League?
    a) 43
    b) 44
    c) 45

20. Who was the oldest player to appear in the Premier League in 2011/12?
    a) Brad Friedel
    b) Radek Cerny
    c) Mark Schwarzer

Answers to Quiz 86: Pot Luck

1. Manchester United
2. Berne in Switzerland
3. Manchester City
4. Dennis Bailey
5. Jens Lehmann
6. Aston Villa, Everton and Blackburn Rovers
7. A cat
8. Preston North End and Huddersfield Town
9. Graham Alexander
10. Gary Ablett
11. Nigeria
12. John Pantsil
13. Nick Barmby, Craig Bellamy, Marcus Bent, Andy Cole, Les Ferdinand, Peter Crouch and Robbie Keane
14. Gary Lineker
15. Gillingham
16. Andrey Arshavin
17. Trevor Hockey
18. Elgin City
19. The ref suffered an allergic reaction to a bee sting
20. 108

DIFFICULT

Quiz 88: Pot Luck

1. The record victory in an FA Cup final is 6-0. Who were the winners?

2. Which Brazilian legend's nickname translates into English as The Wren?

3. True or false – In the 1960s Stoke City played in a pro league in America under the name of the Cleveland Stokers?

4. What nationality is Wigan's Jean Beausejour?

5. What are the only three clubs to have won the European Cup, Cup Winners' Cup and Uefa Cup?

6. Seven countries have been runners-up in the World Cup more than once. Can you name them?

7. Which three Aston Villa players have been named PFA Player of the Year?

8. Simon Garner is which club's all-time leading goalscorer?

9. Which team beat West Germany in home and away qualifiers for Euro 84 but still didn't reach the finals?

10. Which combative Italian midfielder liked to prepare for a match by reading a passage from a Dostoevsky novel?

11. Which manager has won all three UEFA club trophies as well as league titles in Italy, Germany, Portugal and Austria?

12. Eight English clubs have only ever played in the top two divisions. Can you name them?

13. Who won championship-winning medals with Everton in 1985 and Arsenal in 1989?

14. Who are the only club to have won all four English divisions, the FA Cup, the League Cup and the Football League Trophy?

15. Which team were knocked out of the 1974 World Cup after the group stage despite being the only team in the tournament not to lose a match?

16. Diego Maradona played for which three European clubs?

17. Which England Test cricketer was also a member of England's 1950 World Cup squad?

18. Which two Irish goalkeeping brothers were on opposing teams in a 1990 match between Bury and Preston?

19. Which Premier League striker has the middle name Cyril?
    a) Darren Bent
    b) Kevin Davies
    c) Peter Crouch

20. How many Laws of Association Football are there?
    a) 17
    b) 27
    c) 37

Answers to Quiz 87: Premier League

1. Norwich City
2. Tony Yeboah
3. Kevin Campbell
4. Nathan Blake and Herman Hreidarsson
5. Oleg Luzhny
6. Marc Albrighton
7. QPR
8. Andrei Kanchelskis, Andrei Arshavin and Pavel Pogrebnyak
9. Shaun Goater and Kyle Lightbourne
10. Ian Branfoot
11. Ryan Giggs, Paul Scholes, Gary Neville, Steven Gerrard and Jamie Carragher
12. Christopher Wreh
13. Ron Atkinson and Kevin Keegan
14. Swindon Town
15. West Bromwich Albion in 2004/05
16. 3rd by Newcastle in 1993/94 and Nottingham Forest in 1994/95
17. Portsmouth and Reading
18. Crystal Palace
19. 45
20. Brad Friedel

DIFFICULT

Quiz 89: Goalscorers

1. Who is the only man to score against Manchester United in the Premier League for four different clubs?

2. Which former Ajax, Barcelona and Liverpool striker's international career spanned four decades?

3. Who is the only Scot to play for Barcelona?

4. Which much-travelled lower league striker, who scored 173 goals in 752 league appearances, was nicknamed The Chief?

5. Didier Drogba joined Chelsea from which club?

6. Which Englishman has scored the most Premier League goals without playing for the national team?

7. Craig Madden is the all-time leading league goalscorer with which north-west club?

8. Which veteran Bournemouth striker, who was still playing in 2012, had a stand at Dean Court named after him that year?

9. With 434 goals between 1947 and 1965, who is the leading goalscorer in English football history?

10. Who scored over 1,000 goals for Vasco da Gama, Barcelona, PSV Eindhoven, Valencia and Brazil?

11. Who holds the record for the most goals in a single World Cup tournament and how many did he score?

12. Who scored in five consecutive England appearances between November 1981 and June 1982?

13. Which Frenchman scored the first-ever Golden Goal in a World Cup match?

14. Clayton Donaldson was the leading scorer in the Football League in 2010/11. Which club did he play for?

15. How many goals did Geoff Hurst score in the 1966 World Cup?

16. Who was the last player to score 50 goals in a season for an English league club?

17. Who scored nine goals in an FA Cup-1st round win for Bournemouth in 1970?

18. Which three players scored hat tricks for Manchester City in their 10-1 win over Huddersfield in 1987?

19. Who was the last player to score four goals for England in a single game?
    a) Les Ferdinand
    b) Alan Shearer
    c) Ian Wright

20. German goal machine Gerd Müller played 62 games for Germany. How many goals did he score?
    a) 64
    b) 66
    c) 68

Answers to Quiz 88: Pot Luck

1. Bury
2. Garrincha
3. True
4. Chilean
5. Bayern Munich, Ajax and Juventus
6. Argentina, Czechoslovakia, Hungary, Brazil, Germany, Italy and Holland
7. Andy Gray, Paul McGrath and David Platt
8. Blackburn Rovers
9. Northern Ireland
10. Gennaro Gattuso
11. Giovanni Trapattoni
12. Arsenal, Chelsea, Everton, Liverpool, Manchester United, Newcastle United, Tottenham Hotspur and West Ham United
13. Kevin Richardson
14. Wolverhampton Wanderers
15. Scotland
16. Barcelona, Napoli and Sevilla
17. Willie Watson
18. Alan and Gary Kelly
19. Kevin Davies
20. 17

DIFFICULT

Quiz 90: Pot Luck

1. In 2002/03, a team from which university reached the FA Cup 1st round proper?

2. Who was the first Australian to gain a Premier League winner's medal?

3. Can you name three post war-England internationals whose surname contains three Os?

4. Which European Cup-winning club is nicknamed Godenzonen (Sons of the Gods)?

5. What name comes next in this list – Howard Kendall, Mike Walker, Joe Royle…?

6. Former Newcastle, Aston Villa and West Ham midfielder Nolberto Solana is an accomplished player of which musical instrument?

7. Which two stadiums have hosted both the men's and women's World Cup final?

8. Which club has the dubious honour of being relegated from the English top flight the most times?

9. Who were the first side to start a Premier League match without any British players?

10. Five England internationals have played in the European Cup / Champions League final with a foreign club. Can you name them?

11. What is the smallest country to reach the quarterfinals of the World Cup?

12. Who was the last Welsh captain to lift the FA Cup?

13. Who was the first footballer to gain 10 million followers on Twitter?

14. In 2007, which American-born player became the first amateur to play for the Republic of Ireland for over 40 years?

15. Who made a record-breaking 683 League appearances for Portsmouth between 1978 and 2000, the most by a goalkeeper for any single club?

16. In 1983, the Football League was sponsored for the first time, by which company?

17. In what decade was shirt-numbering made compulsory?

18. Why was Everton's Premier League match against Man City in February 2012 interrupted?

19. Between 1872 and 1929 Scotland played 43 matches against England, Scotland and Ireland. How many did they lose?
    a) 2
    b) 4
    c) 6

20. What does the tactical term Catenaccio mean in English?
    a) door bolt
    b) iron gate
    c) fortress

Answers to Quiz 89: Goalscorers

1. Les Ferdinand
2. Jari Litmanen (1989 to 2010)
3. Steve Archibald
4. Wayne Allison
5. Marseille
6. Kevin Campbell
7. Bury
8. Steve Fletcher
9. Arthur Rowley
10. Romario
11. Just Fontaine (13)
12. Paul Mariner
13. Laurent Blanc
14. Crewe Alexandra
15. 4
16. Steve Bull
17. Ted MacDougall
18. Tony Adcock, Paul Stewart and David White
19. Ian Wright
20. 68

DIFFICULT

Quiz 91: Family Ties

1. Who were the first father and son to gain Premier League winner's medals?

2. John Bond and son Kevin both had spells as manager of which Football League club?

3. Which brothers played for Manchester United in the 1977 FA Cup final?

4. Can you name the five pairs of brothers that played in the Premier League in 2009/10?

5. Which England international is the uncle of goalscorer and broadcaster Jason Roberts?

6. What is the name of Eric Cantona's brother who had brief spells at Peterborough and Stockport County?

7. Which three brothers played for Southampton against Sheffield Wednesday in 1988?

8. What is the name of Xabi Alonso's brother who had a brief spell at Bolton?

9. In the opening game of the 1990 World Cup, one brother was sent off and the other scored the winner. Which brothers?

10. Which England defender's brother had spells at Yeovil and Leyton Orient between 2003 and 2009?

11. Which twins played together at Bolton then faced off against each other as managers in the Conference in 2010?

12. Which defender won one cap for England in 1967 while his brother earned 11 caps for Wales?

13. Which Chilean brothers played for Newcastle in the 1950s?

14. Which father and son lifted the European Cup in 1963 and 2003 respectively?

15. In a 1996 international, which father was substituted and replaced by his son?

16. Which brothers played in the 1975 European Cup final?

17. The son of which England captain made over 30 appearances for Blackpool in 2011/12?

18. Which brothers, who played for Manchester City in the 1990s, are the sons of Olympic champion Ann Packer?

19. Who is the son-in-law of Dutch manager Bert van Marwijk?
    a) Mark van Bommel
    b) Arjen Robben
    c) Robin van Persie

20. Which one of the following is a brother of Clive Allen?
    a) Bradley
    b) Martin
    c) Paul

Answers to Quiz 90: Pot Luck

1. Bath University
2. Robbie Slater
3. Peter Osgood, Ian Storey-Moore and Tony Woodcock
4. Ajax Amsterdam
5. Howard Kendall (again)
6. Trumpet
7. Rose Bowl, Pasadena and Rasunda Stadium, Stockholm
8. Birmingham City
9. Chelsea
10. Kevin Keegan, Laurie Cunningham, Chris Waddle, Steve McManaman and Owen Hargreaves
11. Northern Ireland
12. Everton's Kevin Ratcliffe
13. Kaka
14. Joe Lapira
15. Alan Knight
16. Canon
17. 1930s
18. A man handcuffed himself to the posts
19. 2
20. Door bolt

DIFFICULT

Quiz 92: Pot Luck

1. Who, in 1998, became the first player to lose Wembley FA Cup finals with three clubs?
2. Three players have won the European Football of the Year award three times. Can you name them?
3. Who was the first Arsenal player to score in a competitive match at the Emirates Stadium?
4. Newcastle United beat which Hungarian side to win the 1969 Fairs Cup?
5. Who was the first manager from outside the British Isles to lead an English club side out in a Wembley cup final?
6. Can you name six players who have scored Premier League hat tricks whose first and last names start with the same letter?
7. Who were the only two outfield players (both at Merseyside clubs) to play every minute of the 2010/11 Premier League season?
8. In what year did the first all-Merseyside League Cup final take place?
9. In 2001/02, all three newly promoted teams avoided relegation from the Premier League. Who were the three teams?
10. What is the only country to win the World Cup despite not winning any of its first round games?
11. What is the name of the central character in the Goal! series of films?
12. Who is the only Spanish-born player to win the European Footballer of the Year award?
13. Name two Scottish players to have played in European Cup finals for non-British clubs?
14. Which five Scottish clubs start and end with the same letter?
15. Who played for Leeds in the 1975 European Cup final and Nottingham Forest in the 1980 final?
16. Which South American manager was banned from football for two months in 2009 after a foul-mouthed rant at journalists?

17. The name of which Scottish team doesn't contain any of the letters from the word football?
18. Which goalkeeper went 517 minutes without conceding a goal in the 1990 World Cup?
19. Field Marshal Montgomery was the honorary President of which club?
    a) Brighton
    b) Portsmouth
    c) Southampton
20. Which club has spent the most seasons in the second tier of English football?
    a) Barnsley
    b) Bradford
    c) Hull City

Answers to Quiz 91: Family Ties

1. Ian Wright and Shaun Wright-Phillips
2. Bournemouth
3. Jimmy and Brian Greenhoff
4. Gary and Phil Neville, Fabio and Rafael da Silva, Rio and Anton Ferdinand, Michael and Andy Dawson, Gary and Steven Caldwell
5. Cyrille Regis
6. Joel
7. Danny, Rod and Ray Wallace
8. Mikel Alonso
9. Andre Kana-Biyik and Francois Oman-Biyik
10. Paul Terry, brother of John
11. Dean and David Holdsworth
12. John and Dave Hollins
13. George and Ted Robledo
14. Cesare and Paolo Maldini
15. Arnor Gudjohnsen was replaced by Eidur
16. Frank and Eddie Gray
17. Paul Ince (his son is Tom Ince)
18. David and Ian Brightwell
19. Mark van Bommel
20. Bradley

DIFFICULT

Quiz 93: Original Names

Can you identify the current English clubs from their original names?

1. Pine Villa

2. Dial Square

3. Shaddongate United

4. Belmont AFC

5. Singers FC

6. Christ Church FC

7. New Brompton

8. Ardwick FC

9. Headington

10. St Jude's

11. The Black Arabs

12. Stanley

13. Newton Heath

14. Thornhill United

15. St Mary's Young Men's Association

DIFFICULT

16. Riverside FC

17. Glyn Cricket and Football Club

18. St Luke's

19. Heaton Norris Rovers

20. Thames Iron Works FC

Answers to Quiz 92: Pot Luck

1. John Barnes (Watford, Liverpool and Newcastle)

2. Johan Cruyff, Michel Platini and Marco van Basten

3. Gilberto Silva

4. Ujpest

5. Stockport County's Danny Bergara

6. Afonso Alves, Andrei Arshavin, Didier Drogba, Dion Dublin, Efan Ekoku and Pavel Pogrebnyak.

7. Leighton Baines and Martin Skrtel

8. 1984

9. Blackburn, Bolton and Fulham

10. Italy in 1982

11. Santiago Munez

12. Luis Suarez in 1960

13. Paul Lambert and Steve Archibald

14. East Stirlingshire, Celtic, Dundee United, Kilmarnock, and East Fife

15. Frank Gray

16. Diego Maradona

17. Dundee

18. Walter Zenga

19. Portsmouth

20. Barnsley

DIFFICULT

Quiz 94: Pot Luck

1. Which three player-managers have taken part in an FA Cup Final?

2. In the 2010/11 season, which club completed the double over Liverpool for the first time since 1946/47?

3. Peter Beardsley's final Football League appearance was with which club?

4. Who is Italy's most capped international player?

5. What was the final score in the football match in the film Escape To Victory?

6. The Pichichi is an award given to the leading scorer in which country?

7. Who are the two World Cup winners to have managed Chelsea?

8. What is the smallest country that is a member of UEFA?

9. Which Manchester City winger, who has had loan spells at Rangers, Bolton and Espanyol, is the third generation of his family to play international football?

10. Which teams take part in a derby match called the Superclasico?

11. Who scored 149 Premier League goals, none of which came from the penalty spot?

12. Arthur Antunes Coimbra is the real name of which Brazilian player and manager?

13. Who was the first Swedish player to win the Premier League?

14. Which club has spent the most seasons in the top flight without winning the league?

15. Who were the first country to qualify for six World Cups without being a host country or a defending champion?

16. Alex Ferguson's first game in charge of Manchester United ended in a 2-0 defeat at the hands of which club?

17. Which three World Cup-winning players have managed in the Premier League?

18. What number shirt did Ossie Ardiles wear at the 1982 World Cup?

19. Which English football club's kit is based on the colours of the Prince of Wales Own Regiment of Yorkshire?
a) Bradford City
b) Huddersfield Town
c) Sheffield United

20. How many players did Aston Villa use in their 1980/81 League Championship winning season?
a) 14
b) 15
c) 16

Answers to Quiz 93: Original Names

1. Oldham Athletic
2. Arsenal
3. Carlisle United
4. Tranmere Rovers
5. Coventry City
6. Bolton Wanderers
7. Gillingham
8. Manchester City
9. Oxford United
10. QPR
11. Bristol Rovers
12. Newcastle United
13. Manchester United
14. Rotherham United
15. Southampton
16. Cardiff City
17. Leyton Orient
18. Wolverhampton Wanderers
19. Stockport County
20. West Ham United

DIFFICULT

Quiz 95: Club Names

In which country will you find the following clubs?

1. Newell's Old Boys

2. Leon de Huanuco

3. Orlando Pirates

4. Velez Sarsfield

5. Hearts of Oak

6. Everton de Viña del Mar

7. Lov Ham

8. Insurance Management Bears

9. Young Boys Berne

10. Germinal Beerschot

11. Zalaegerszegi Torna Egylet

12. NAC Breda

13. Fotballaget Fart

14. Club Always Ready

15. The New Saints

Answers - page 197

16. Go Ahead Eagles

17. FC BATE Borisov

18. CFR Cluj

19. Hércules CF

20. Bohemians

Answers to Quiz 94: Pot Luck

1. Kenny Dalglish, Glenn Hoddle and Dennis Wise
2. Blackpool
3. Hartlepool United
4. Fabio Cannovaro
5. 4-all
6. Spain
7. Luiz Felipe Scolari and Geoff Hurst
8. San Marino
9. Vladimir Weiss
10. River Plate and Boca Juniors
11. Les Ferdinand
12. Zico
13. Jesper Blomqvist
14. Bolton Wanderers
15. Belgium
16. Oxford United
17. Ossie Ardiles, Alan Ball and Karl-Heinz Riedle
18. 1
19. Bradford City
20. 14

DIFFICULT

Quiz 96: Pot Luck

1. Which two goalkeepers have captained a team to an FA Cup final victory?

2. What is the only club to reach a major English cup final while playing in the bottom division?

3. When Liverpool beat Crystal Palace 9-0 in 1989 there were eight different scorers. Which Scot was the only player to score twice?

4. Who was the first South American player to receive a Premier League winner's medal?

5. Who scored England's goal in their 4-1 drubbing by Germany at the 2010 World Cup?

6. Chris Waddle enjoyed a brief spell at which Scottish club?

7. Which Barnsley striker scored, missed a penalty and was sent off, within five minutes in a game at Sunderland in 1998?

8. The Mestalla Stadium is the home ground of which Spanish club?

9. Which four prime ministers were mentioned in the famous 'your boys took a hell of a beating' speech after England's loss to Norway in 1982?

10. Which country came third in both the 1974 and 1982 World Cups?

11. Which country once went 9 hours, 18 minutes without conceding a World Cup finals goal?

12. Even though England didn't qualify for 2008, two English-born players appeared at the finals. Can you name them?

13. Which two South American teams took part in the first international match outside the British Isles?

14. Six players have top flight-winner's medals from the old Division One and the Premier League. Can you name them?

15. The 2012 Europa League final was held in which city?

16. Which three Football League clubs contain all the letters from the word goal in their name?

17. Roy Hodgson's first managerial job in England was with which club?

18. What was the only country to make its European Championships debut in the 2012 tournament?

19. Which of the following clubs hasn't won the Football League Trophy twice?
a) Bristol City
b) Port Vale
c) Wolves

20. Newcastle United's Jonas Gutierrez has what unusual hobby?
a) paleontology
b) campanology
c) philately

Answers to Quiz 95: Club Names

1.	Argentina	11.	Hungary
2.	Peru	12.	Holland
3.	South Africa	13.	Norway
4.	Argentina	14.	Bolivia
5.	Ghana	15.	Wales
6.	Chile	16.	Holland
7.	Norway	17.	Belarus
8.	Bahamas	18.	Romania
9.	Switzerland	19.	Spain
10.	Belgium	20.	Ireland

DIFFICULT

Quiz 97: Managers part 2

1. Which former Brighton, Swindon and Southend defender was the first black manager of an England representative team?

2. Who was appointed manager of Lincoln City in 1972 at the age of just 28?

3. Which two managers have been awarded honorary OBEs for their 'contribution to football and Franco-British relations'?

4. Who had spells managing Aston Villa and Manchester City in 1986/87, a season that saw both clubs relegated from the top flight?

5. Which Scottish national team manager shares his name with a bad boy soul singer?

6. Who led Chelsea to their first top flight title in 1955?

7. Which former England defender took charge of Notts County in 2012?

8. Who steered Argentina to glory in the 1978 World Cup?

9. Alex Ferguson's middle name is the same as the surname of a former Leeds United striker. What is it?

10. Up to the start of the 2011/12 season, only five bosses had managed in 1,000 league games. Can you name them?

11. Who was named manager of Torquay United in May 2007 but was sacked ten minutes later when new owners took charge of the club?

12. Who was the manager of the England women's team at the 2011 World Cup?

13. Who was appointed director of football at Crawley Town in April 2012?

14. Which much-travelled player-turned-pundit was in charge at Millwall for 36 days in 2005?

15. Sheffield Wednesday boss Dave Jones started his managerial career at which club?

16. Who was the first black manager in English football and what club did he manage?

17. Which manager has had spells in charge at York City, Bristol Rovers, Bristol City, Wolves, Cheltenham, Carlisle and most recently, Colchester United?

18. Who was the first player-manager in England's top flight?

19. In 2003, which club chose its manager by a telephone poll of players, fans and shareholders?
    a) Grimsby Town
    b) Lincoln City
    c) Luton Town

20. Who is the longest-serving manager with a single club in Scottish football history?
    a) Jim McLean
    b) Walter Smith
    c) Jock Stein

Answers to Quiz 96: Pot Luck

1. Dave Beasant and David Seaman
2. Rochdale (in the League Cup in 1962)
3. Steve Nicol
4. Edu
5. Matthew Upson
6. Falkirk
7. Ashley Ward
8. Valencia
9. Sir Winston Churchill, Sir Anthony Eden, Clement Attlee, Maggie Thatcher
10. Poland
11. Switzerland
12. Simone Perrotta and Colin Kazim-Richards
13. Argentina and Uruguay
14. Tony Adams, Steve Bould, Lee Dixon, David Seaman, Nigel Winterburn and Eric Cantona
15. Bucharest
16. Accrington Stanley, Brighton & Hove Albion, Plymouth Argyle
17. Bristol City
18. Ukraine
19. Wolves
20. Paleontology

DIFFICULT

Quiz 98: Pot Luck

1. What was the last all-English team to win the FA Cup final?

2. Which Liverpool player appeared on the cover of The Beatles' Sergeant Pepper album?

3. Prior to 2011, when was the last time that two teams ending in City met in an FA Cup final?

4. Which four English players have won the European Footballer of the Year award?

5. Who was the first full-time Wigan Athletic player to be capped by England?

6. Chris Birchall, Port Vale's most capped player, plays international football for which country?

7. Only nine clubs have won the Spanish league title. Can you name them?

8. Who did Michel Platini succeed as head of UEFA?

9. Who is the only English player to have scored in FA Cup, League Cup, UEFA Cup and Champions League finals?

10. Rangers won nine consecutive SPL titles between 1989 and 1997. Can you name the four players who played in all nine title-winning sides?

11. Which three English Aston Villa players have also played for Bari in Italy?

12. What was the name of the England squad's official 1986 World Cup song?

13. The first player from mainland Europe to score in the Premier League is now the manager of MLS team Columbus Crew. What is his name?

14. Which Scot had a spell playing in Serie A for AC Milan and Verona?

15. What is the only club to appear in a Champions League final without ever having won their domestic league?

16. Who is Argentina's all-time leading international goalscorer?

17. Which Polish footballer, who had a spell at Manchester City, appeared in the film Escape To Victory?

18. Who were the first sponsors of the FA Cup?

19. Luigi Riva is Italy's all-time leading international goalscorer. How many goals did he score?
    a) 35
    b) 45
    c) 55

20. Panamanian footballer Luis Moreno was given a two-game ban after kicking what stray animal from the pitch during Deportivo Pereira's game against Junior Barranquilla?
    a) dog
    b) fox
    c) owl

Answers to Quiz 97: Managers part 2

1. Chris Ramsey, who was in charge of the U20s in 1999
2. Graham Taylor
3. Arsene Wenger and Gerard Houllier
4. Billy McNeill
5. Bobby Brown
6. Ted Drake
7. Keith Curle
8. Cesar Luis Menotti
9. Chapman
10. Alec Stock, Jim Smith, Brian Clough, Graham Taylor and Dario Gradi
11. Leroy Rosenior
12. Hope Powell
13. Steve Coppell
14. Steve Claridge
15. Stockport County
16. Tony Collins at Rochdale from 1960 to 1968
17. John Ward
18. QPR's Les Allen
19. Luton Town
20. Jim McLean with Dundee United

DIFFICULT

Quiz 99: Grounds and Stadiums

Which non-British clubs play at the following grounds?

1. Estádio José Alvalade

2. Dalymount Park

3. Stadio Artemio Franchi

4. Estadio San Mamés

5. Westfalenstadion

6. Constant Vanden Stock Stadium

7. Stade Geoffroy-Guichard

8. Franz Horr Stadion

9 İnönü Stadium

10. Stadion Albert Flórián

11. Estadio Monumental Antonio Vespucio Liberti

12. Stadio San Paolo

13. Volksparkstadion

14. Rat Verlegh Stadion

15. Estadio La Rosaleda (The Rose Garden)

DIFFICULT

Answers - page 205

16. Stade Chaban-Delmas (formerly Parc Lescure)

17. Stade Louis II

18. Donbas Arena

19. Karaiskakis Stadium

20. Şükrü Saracoğlu Stadium

Answers to Quiz 98: Pot Luck

1. West Ham in 1975
2. Albert Stubbins
3. 1969 Man City v Leicester City
4. Stanley Matthews, Bobby Charlton, Kevin Keegan and Michael Owen
5. Emile Heskey (Chris Kirkland was on loan from Liverpool when he was capped)
6. Trinidad and Tobago
7. Real Madrid, Barcelona, Atletico Madrid, Athletic Bilbao, Valencia, Real Sociedad, Deportivo La Coruna, Sevilla and Real Betis
8. Lennart Johansson
9. Steven Gerrard
10. Richard Gough, Ally McCoist, Ian Ferguson and Ian Durrant
11. Gordon Cowans, Paul Rideout and David Platt
12. We've Got The Whole World At Our Feet
13. Robert Warzycha
14. Joe Jordan
15. Bayer Leverkusen
16. Gabriel Batistuta
17. Kazimierz Deyna
18. Littlewoods
19. 35
20. Owl

DIFFICULT

Quiz 100: Pot Luck

1. Which Russian is the only player to score five goals in a single World Cup finals match?

2. Which two teams qualified for the 2012 European Championships with a 100% record?

3. Who are the five players to have scored over 100 Premier League goals, all of them coming while playing at a single club?

4. Which two players have scored for both Liverpool and Everton in Merseyside derby games?

5. With spells at Manchester United and Hull City, who is the only Angolan to have played in the Premier League?

6. Up to 2012, five Scottish players had scored Premier League hat tricks. Can you name them?

7. Who were the only non-Spanish team to reach the 2012 Europa League semifinal?

8. Which England striker used a drill to treat a blood blister and ended up with a blood infection?

9. Which Northern Irish club play at a ground called Solitude?

10. Who are the seven managers to have completed the clean sweep of top-flight league win, FA Cup win and League Cup win?

11. Which South American club play at La Bombonera?

12. Manuel Francisco dos Santos was the real name of which Brazilian legend?

13. Who holds the record for the most goals in a single European Championships qualifying campaign?

14. Robert Green famously fumbled a shot from which American striker into the net at the 2010 World Cup?

15. Ahmed Hassan, the most capped player in international football, plays for which country?

16. Manchester United won the 2008 World Club Championship after beating a team from which country in the final?

17. Why was Cameroon goalkeeping coach Thomas Nkono arrested minutes before an Africa Cup of Nations semifinal in 2002?

18. What is the oldest surviving international football tournament in the world?

19. How many nationalities were involved in Blackburn's game against West Brom in Jan 2011?
    a) 20
    b) 21
    c) 22

20. Which English club has not won the Welsh Cup?
    a) Chester City
    b) Crewe Alexandra
    c) Stockport County

Answers to Quiz 99: Grounds and Stadiums

1. Sporting Lisbon
2. Bohemians
3. Fiorentina
4. Athletic Bilbao
5. Borussia Dortmund
6. Anderlecht
7. St Etienne
8. Austria Vienna
9. Besiktas
10. Ferencvaros
11. River Plate
12. Napoli
13. Hamburg
14. NAC Breda
15. Malaga
16. Bordeaux
17. Monaco
18. Shakhtar Donetsk
19. Olympiacos
20. Fenerbahçe

DIFFICULT

Keeping Score

Keeping Score

Keeping Score

Keeping Score

Keeping Score

Keeping Score

Keeping Score

Keeping Score

Keeping Score

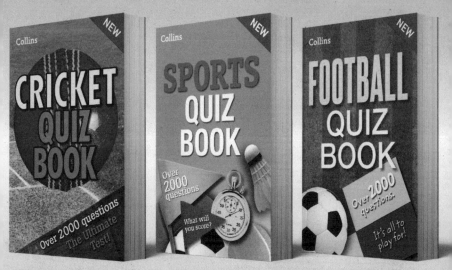